KU-496-870

Michelle Cliff

FREE ENTERPRISE

PENGUIN BOOKS

PENGUIN BOOKS

Published by the Penguin Group
Penguin Books Ltd, 27 Wrights Lane, London W8 5TZ, England
Penguin Books USA Inc., 375 Hudson Street, New York, New York 10014, U.S.A.
Penguin Books Australia Ltd, Ringwood, Victoria, Australia
Penguin Books Canada Ltd, 10 Alcorn Avenue, Toronto, Ontario, Canada M4V 3B2
Penguin Books (N.Z.) Ltd, 182–190 Wairau Road, Auckland 10, New Zealand

Penguin Books Ltd, Registered Offices: Harmondsworth, Middlesex, England

First published in the USA by Dutton, an imprint of New American Library,
a division of Penguin Books USA Inc., 1993
First published in Great Britain by Viking 1994
Published in Penguin Books 1995

1 3 5 7 9 10 8 6 4 2

Copyright © Michelle Cliff, 1993
All rights reserved

The moral right of the author has been asserted

Printed in the USA

Except in the United States of America, this book is sold subject
to the condition that it shall not, by way of trade or otherwise, be lent,
re-sold, hired out, or otherwise circulated without the publisher's
prior consent in any form of binding or cover other than that in
which it is published and without a similar condition including this
condition being imposed on the subsequent purchaser

For Gloria I. Joseph

PENGUIN BOOKS
FREE ENTERPRISE

'*Free Enterprise*, which has as its ambition the rescuing of the past from oblivion, succeeds and more than succeeds—the scorched and scorching world of slavery it resurrects makes the world we now live in seem pale and fragile, like a thin veil tearing: even as Michelle Cliff's illumination of our past helps explain the turbulent and disturbing world we have inherited and now so unquielty live in.'—Susan Fromberg Schaeffer, author of *The Madness of a Seduced Woman* and *First Nights*

'Resonant . . . a subtly powerful story of friendship . . . Cliff has forged an unsentimental language of courage and, if not redemption, then at least protest.' —*Voice Literary Supplement*

'An elegant, elliptical, and highly wrought mosaic of the past that reflects intensely on our present.' —Baltimore *City Paper*

'Alluring . . . an absorbing tale of friendship, survival, and courage.'—*Publishers Weekly*

Michelle Cliff, born in Jamaica, is the author of two previous novels, *Abeng* and *No Telephone to Heaven*; a collection of short stories, *Bodies of Water*; a prose and poetry collection, *The Land of Look Behind*, and a collection of prose poems, *Claiming an Identity They Taught Me to Despise*. She lives in Santa Cruz, California.

Contents

That which is, already has been; that which is to be, already has been; and God seeks what has been driven away.

—ECCLESIASTES 3:15

I always listen for what I can leave out.

—MILES DAVIS

I.

ANNIE
CHRISTMAS

Gens Inconnu

The house almost slid off the land to the south of Carville, hanging on to a spit for dear life. Secluded, as she liked it. Rundown, which didn't faze her; in fact, spoke in its favor.

"You'd have to be crazy to live there," her friends at Carville said when she described the place. She hadn't had the heart to say at least she could come and go. Didn't wear a number for a name.

To their minds, she didn't have very far to go crazy. Weren't her faithful visits evidence of an unbalanced soul?

"Who in their right mind?" they asked each other.

On the very edge—she and the house. Hand to mouth. A disgraceful old age from where her people stood. She who had been born to better things, a better class of people.

The year is 1920. Long time now she'd turned her back

on all that, causing all manner of grief, which she could remember now with remarkably little effort. She'd considered the break clean, but it haunted her.

Who could say why she'd been able to turn her back, when her brothers and sisters took so effortlessly to their places? It didn't matter.

She'd done it. She'd lived her life on the edge, which is where most people who won't settle end up, for good or ill.

She wondered how many wrecked-looking, secluded, vine-tangled places were home to people like herself, when gossip and tradition pertained only to the town's drunk, madman, person with some deep, dark secret, set apart from normal life.

Deformed child tied to a bed in a back room; Mamà's skeleton hanging from the eaves, shreds of a housedress shrouding her.

Annie's house departed from the usual hermitage in one respect. In front, forming a crescent, were live oak and mimosa and cypress trees, each branch bearing bottles she had fixed there herself. Live oak and mimosa and cypress decked with colored glass, clear glass, between her and the river. The Old Man. The Big Muddy. The Father of Waters.

The artery her namesake drained with one kiss. But that's getting ahead of the story, or behind.

Trees adorned with Moxie. Dr Pepper. Royal Crown. Milk of Magnesia. Frank's Louisiana Hot Sauce. Coca-Cola. Jamaica Ginger Beer. Electric Bitters. Lea & Perrin. Hood's Nerve Tonic. Major Grey. Sal Hepatica. Aunt

Sally's Witch Hazel. Bogle's Bay Rum. Mr. Bones's Liquid Blackener. Khus-Khus Original African Scent.

A chaos of residue haloed the trees, scenting the river's mist. Curatives and purgatives and thirst quenchers and condiments and perfumes.

Ingredients from here, there, and everywhere.

She'd scrubbed the bottles with the waters of the Mississippi but to no avail, a babel of scents dwelled in the new moon in front of her house.

She stroked the Khus-Khus bottle as you would stroke the magic lamp. She put her nostrils against it. With its essence some of her ghosts were raised, and she was at a house party, on a July night, the dark perfume rising from a wicker loveseat on a verandah in Runaway Bay, on an island to the south.

The Original African Scent took her upstairs, was enlacing itself in a coverlet pieced by a slave. Annie was there, she could see herself, framed by the four tall posts of a mahogany bedstead, each capped by the headdress of a cacique, the posts trompe l'oeil sugarcane. She was on top of the filigreed coverlet, as the warm breezes, her own breath, swept the Khus-Khus from one corner of the room to another.

On that bed at that moment the entire history of the island could be captured. Arawak. Slavery. Cane. And herself, lying on that bed, having served the landowner well.

Father, uncle, cousin, family friend—what did it matter?

Had it happened?

With Mamà's blessing.

Remember Mamà? *Une femme de gens inconnu?*

Which is what the judgment finally said, in those words, even though the colony was English.

They inhabited a confused universe, this Caribbean, with no center and no outward edge. Where almost everything was foreign. Language, people, landscape even.

Tongues collided. Struggled for hegemony. Emerged victorious, or sank into the impossibly blue waters, heavy as gold.

French was the preference among some people.

For a few a choice made with nostalgia for Toussaint, a casting back to the great house aflame, Dessalines's "Leave nothing white alive!," Christophe's scorched earth, and bust of *Comédie Française,* female, white, in the ruined courtyard of his castle *Sans Souci.*

The eyeflash, when *liberté, égalité, fraternité,* extended even to the Black Jacobins.

Extended to Marie-Guilhelmine Benoist's *Négresse,* hanging in the Paris Salon of 1800. The Antillean sitter with one breast bare. In 1794, *une citoyenne;* in 1802, slave again. In the eyeflash, this. *Moi égal à toi.*

These were the few.

Other enthusiasts sought sophistication, fashion, *une langue civil,* distance from the grubbiness of the trader— who knew only English. These were the sort who would construct a replica of *Sacré-Coeur* in the Martiniquaise jungle, set vineyards on the *soufrière* of Pelée, emb a floor in a chateau on tiny Marie Galante with golden louis d'ors, pried up coin by coin by an enterprising slave by moonlight, whispering, in a litany, *"Article Trente-cinq: Quand le gouvernement viole les droits du peuple, l'insurrection est pour le peuple, et pour chaque portion du peuple, le plus sacré des droits et le plus indispensable des devoirs."*

Over and over, as he pried loose coin upon coin, he spoke these words, establishing, as he worked, into the night, the royal silhouette filling the sack beside him, the new revolutionary currency, every man for himself, and the devil take the hindmost.

English had no such mysteriousness, revolutionary or otherwise. English was the tongue of commerce, the marketplace with its bustle and terror, the harbor crammed with men-of-war rainbowed by flying fish and schooners with their bills of lading in precise, elegant script. Papers signed and sealed by members of the Association for Promoting the Discovery of the Inland Districts of Africa or the Company of Royal Adventurers of England Trading into Africa. Account books bound in Moroccan leather, as weighty as the First Folio. The business of English was business, at least in these waters.

Spanish was the language of the categories. Spanish described the populations of the New World under the imperial gaze. Spanish was terribly concerned with *limpieza de sangre*. Spanish determined that the offspring of a Spaniard and an Albino woman would be *Torna atrás* [a Throwback]; that the offspring of an Indian and a *Torna atrás* woman would be a *Lobo* [Wolf]; that the offspring of a *Lobo* and an Indian woman would be *Zambayo* [Cross-eyed]; that an Indian woman and *Zambayo* man would give birth to a *Tente en el aire* [Suspended in the air]; that a *Tente en el aire* man and a Mulatto woman would have a *No te entiendo* [I don't understand you]; that a *No te entiendo* man and a *Tente en el aire* woman would give life to a *Allí te estás!* [There you are!]

Spanish dispensed the *asiento*, the license to trade.

Latin described the soul. Latin transubstantiated breadfruit to flesh, rum to blood. Latin conveyed the suffering of the Son of God, and our own damnable blame.

Carib Latin did not embrace Ovid or Catullus, but brought home Jerome and Augustine and the martyrdom of St. Catherine in the unbearably bright light, which was the Carib sun.

Hebrew and Chinese and Arabic, oriental and surreptitious, kept mostly to themselves, for reasons of safekeeping, of the language and the people and their varied strangenesses—to the European gaze, of course. The sand on the floor of the synagogue muffled the sounds of the services. The clatter of the abacus in the shop was kept as low as possible, and as short-lived, as the beads sang up and down the columns.

Against these tongues African of every stripe collided. Twi and Mande and Akan and Bambara and Ewe and Fante and Ga and Anyi and Asante and Yoruba and Igbo and Bini. O ba. He comes. O bai. He came. O re ba. He is coming. O be ba. He will come. O a ba. He has come.

African seeped into the parlance of the better class: *le gens inconnu*, trying to trick it into *Jonkonnu*.

The place was a whirlwind.

. . .

Standing one afternoon under several of the flags which had claimed the colony, before the British prevailed once and for all, efficiency conquering all, on the very same verandah in Runaway Bay, Annie's mother made a speech to her.

This time the dominating scent was not Khus-Khus, but the mildew which inevitably followed a downpour, settling into the national silks overhead.

"*Ma fille*," her mother began, "the poor are an investment that will leave you penniless. If you must do this sort of thing, then, for God's sake, become a *religieuse*. Go to France, to a proper convent. Teach the poor to make lace. This business can lead nowhere but heartache, your heartache. Will you lend to the disgrace of us all? Your father and I have worked so hard."

"What sort of disgrace, Mamà?"

"The sort that happens when a daughter turns her back on her people. You belong to us."

Brown. Blue. Cloudy. Green.

Bottles. Eyes.

What on earth would her mother have thought to see her apply Mr. Bones's Liquid Blackener to her carefully inbred skin?

Ye gods.

Talk about disgrace.

It saved her life.

That blackened skin.

Saved her skin.

That blackened life.

She'd turned her back on her people, all right, but not in the way her mother meant it. She fell into the movement on the mainland, believing the island to be without hope.

Believing also, although she hated to admit it, that she was not strong enough to resist on home ground; it overwhelmed her. At least the ground she knew as home, was born to. Divided and planted with feudal exactitude, stonefenced against an impending green. The place was bisected by a limestone aqueduct, drawing water from a sinkhole in the hills above the estate. Because the limestone was mortared with molasses, the water took on a sweetish taste, like everything on the estate, resonant of sugar. Warm, sweet water, drawn from the hills where doctor birds slid their lancet bills into the cups of orchids, and spun nests the size of limes from spider webs. But against this, always, was the overseer's house, set on an eminence overlooking fields and quarters, lending a literalness to his title which served the efficiency of the place, where things ran like clockwork, and the humming of birds was drowned in the crack of the whip.

As soon as she had money of her own, she made tracks. Too many nights on the slave-pieced coverlet, with the promise of many more.

"It is a small price to pay to be secure," her mother assured her, adding some words about a woman's lot in life and the need to make the best of it. With a postscript on having been raised by servants and being ill equipped to enter into negotiation with the world alone.

Like Harriet, and Ellen Craft, and other runaway

women she had come to know, she began her revolting behavior with her own escape.

These many years later she walked alongside her crescent of bottle trees.

The lines of the Coca-Cola bottle were meant to represent the corseted form of a woman, compelled by whalebone almost beyond hope of breath, her bosom straining forward. Looking at the bottle now, in her mood of reminiscence, Annie could see Frances Ellen Watkins Harper tilted over a lectern in 1858, speaking on "The Education and the Elevation of the Colored Race," advocating a Talented Tenth. They'd met but that once, and Annie, questioning from the floor of the Tremont Temple, as Mrs. Harper strained forward to listen, immediately knew she was disapproved of. In her *guise de guerre*, light-years from the stone-enclosed fields, the overseer's eminence, her back turned on *gens inconnu*, Annie may have been too much, too easily typed in Mrs. Harper's talented eyes as one of the nine tenths.

No light-skinned female Christian octoroon she, unlike Iola Leroy, heroine of Mrs. Harper's later runaway best-seller, who finds herself in the pit of slavery, and she a graduate of a fine New England school for ladies, a plot twist guaranteed to wring hearts dry; white ones, at least.

"I do not understand how you can advocate a concept which eliminates the vast majority of our people."

"We are not speaking of elimination" came Mrs. Harper's reply, "but of the necessity of leadership by the exceptional among us."

"There should be no exception made; we are all exceptional, surely" was Annie's heartfelt, and hard-won, response.

"That is a supremely romantic notion, miss. We need be practical. Our people exist in a hostile universe, we have no choice but to accommodate ourselves to its laws."

The exchange had great potential, but its venue was unfortunate, and each woman cut her argument short, loath to wrangle in front of the Bostonian audience in a female version of a battle royal.

Annie returned to her seat near the back of the auditorium, where she caught the eye of another, older woman, one who smiled in her direction, took something from her purse, and passed it through several rows of silent listeners in Annie's direction. It was a calling card, engraved on the front

Mary Ellen Pleasant
1661 Octavia Street
San Francisco
California

On the reverse was written

Would you be my guest for supper this evening?
M.E.P.

Annie read the note, nodded to the woman in response, and met her afterward. To say their meeting changed her life would be the most extreme understatement.

When Annie's mother petitioned as far as the Custos of St. Ann, and won, she threw a great ball. With a huge cake covered all over by the finest slivers of coconut, like the hairs of an old white man, carried into the ballroom on the shoulders of footmen dressed in white silk, a pearl dangling from an ear. The ladies wore gowns decked with albatross feathers, which would have horrified Coleridge, but the islanders had no such taboo. The French doors were flung wide and deadwhite gowns fought the deadwhiteness of a full moon for paleness. In the center of the invading moonlight, a long table, inlaid with squares of Carrara marble, was piled high with hundreds of eggs laid by the masked, red-footed booby, who nested in the black volcanic sands of the beach.

This was all to celebrate becoming *gens inconnu,* which in those days, her mother would have emphasized, meant something.

Once in a blue moon, if the breeze from the river came up in a certain way, and filled the spaces between bottles and branches, there might be a tune. The trees would sing. The glass would a-men. Lamentation or bamboula, or something in between, depending on the heaviness of the air, the mood of the glass, the density of the tree, the capability of the listener.

.   .   .

The year in which Annie makes her progress through her crescent moon of bottle trees on the banks of the Mississippi River is 1920.

So says the calendar on the wall inside her house, which came to her courtesy of the Black Star Shipping Line. Above the numerals, days of the week, phases of the moon, is an artist's rendering of the S.S. *Phillis Wheatley*—imagine it.

With each month, the progress of the ship is imagined, from her baptism in a berth on the Harlem River, to her passage past the Ambrose Light, through the blackness of the Atlantic she plows, her prow slicing the water, glancing white caps, the name of the poet glazed with salt, over burial ground she goes, arriving like Cleopatra, triumphant, amid throngs carrying armsful of fantastic flowers, at the dock to greet her, sweeping her path with palms, offering her baskets of fruit, tottering in their height and fullness, in Accra—Africa achieved, finally, by a ship that never came to be.

Sixty-one years fall between 1858 and 1920. Almost a lifetime. For many, indeed a lifetime.

Plucky Abolitionism

"Plucky abolitionism" was the description given their enterprise by Mary Shadd Carey at the Chatham Convention. It was the courageous stand, she said, her voice filling the Negro schoolhouse where they met, "the difference between word and movement, talk and blood, drawing room and battlefield." Between what she called "passive righteousness" and treading close, threatening, what the white man thought should be in his or his God's or his blasted Union's hands.

"It is the difference, my friends, between being an American liberal and being an American radical.

" 'Arm the Negroes?!' Can you hear them? Can you see them draw back in horror, that they ever trusted us, thought us reasonable in the pursuit of justice? They tremble as they ask us, thinking, perhaps it is Africa showing;

thinking, they have scratched us, and we are savage. They tremble as they ask us, 'Sweet Jesus, do you advocate anarchism?' 'No,' we will respond, 'only zealous commitment to the cause.' And we will leave it at that.

"Whosoever wants may come on board, but we well know that many will not. Only the few will choose to go so far." She paused, and with a glance in their direction, acknowledged Captain Brown and some of his troops. "The few will go with us all the way, and reap whatever we shall reap."

They drew up a constitution for a separate African-American state, and took up arms, beginning their war of independence in October 1859.

And when the smoke cleared the name officially attached to the deed was John Brown.

Who has ever heard of Annie Christmas, Mary Shadd Carey, Mary Ellen Pleasant?

The official version has been printed, bound, and gagged, resides in schools, libraries, the majority unconscious. Serves the common good. Does not cause trouble. Walks across tapestries, the television screen. Does not give aid and comfort to the enemy. Is the stuff of convocations, colloquia; is substantiated—like the Host—in dissertations.

The official version is presented to the people. With friezes of heroes, statues free-standing in vest-pocket parks, in full costume on Main Street, on auditorium stages in elementary schools, through two-reelers, in silence—who will forget *The Birth of a Nation*?

The official version entertains. Illumines the Great White Way. Is hummed along Tin Pan Alley, by song-pluggers eager for a tip. "I'd walk a million miles for one of your smiles." Is barked on the midway at the state fair, alongside the hoochie-koochie girls, the dancing bear. Appears in novels sold for a penny, is serialized in *Harper's Monthly,* in newspapers where the owner sets his own hot type, inks the rollers, feeds the press, waits on the Pulitzer. Is talked over luncheons at the Rotary, Kiwanis, chambers of commerce. Gets top billing on the vaudeville circuit.

The official version is in everybody's mouth. On the lips of toastmasters, chairwomen of garden clubs, the Gold Dust Twins; cluttering dreams, remembered in prayers.

This is what happened; this is how it was.

There would soon enough be no one who knew the real story.

"Frederick, is God dead?" Sojourner Truth asked Douglass.

"No. God is not dead, and therefore slavery must end in blood," Frederick Douglass responded.

And there remain so few who have an inkling of what was meant by that exchange.

"Give it up," M.E.P. had advised, toward the end.

But M.E.P. didn't follow her own advice, inscribing words on her epitaph which would send shivers through some and, at the very best, create doubts about the official version. There it was, in letters blackened in the white slab in a cemetery in a town known for wine in the California countryside:

SHE WAS A FRIEND OF JOHN BROWN

"Mary Ellen Pleasant?"

"Wasn't she a voodoo queen?"

"A madam?"

"A mammy?"

"Didn't she run a whorehouse for white businessmen in San Francisco?"

"Wasn't she Mammy Pleasant?"

"Didn't she work voodoo on that white woman and send her off her head?"

"Wasn't she Haitian?"

"Didn't she have a witch mark on her forehead?"

"A cast eye?"

"One blue eye and one brown eye?"

"Wasn't she ebony?"

"Yellow?"

"Wasn't she so pale you'd never know?"

"Didn't she come back as a zombie?"

"Didn't she have a penis?"

"Couldn't she work roots?"

"Didn't she make a senator's balls fall off?"

"Didn't she set fire to her own house?"

"Never heard of her."

Her "give it up" was meant to ease heartache.

Life on the Mississippi

Never settled, never at home on the continent to the north, even after a lifetime in exile there, Annie Christmas thought of her island each day of her life.

She thought every now and then of returning. Of getting a small boat, packing up some salted fish and beef, a thermos of hot coffee, hardtack, and setting out on the water, drifting down the river, through the delta, across the gulf, and into the wide sargasso sea, never looking back, an eighty-year-old woman rowing with the strength of a young man, her arms becoming suddenly finely muscled, returning to the place of her origin—and to what?

It was her fantasy, and she knew it, that there was a solution to the placelessness which had always been hers, even as a girl behind her mother's skirts.

.   .   .

Her mother's family tree was constructed of mythopoetic tales, seemingly devised to entertain a child rather than form the basis of dynasty. The tree branched into swashbucklers, riders on the Spanish Main, swordsmen, petty nobility, an aide-de-camp to the Duke of Wellington, an Arawak or two—but not the anthropophagic Carib—a female pirate who begged off execution due to motherhood, but never the guineaman, the driver, the cane cutter, the furious Maroon.

Annie was born into this imperial rain forest, and christened Regina (pronounced with a long *i*), which she later discarded. Queendom was not hers.

Last night she'd had a strange dream, about a multicolored snake with a black head. A man in the dream—she couldn't quite make him out—talked about how the snake was being trampled; she, who'd always feared snakes, was in the dream frightened for one. Was she it?

The snake was being trampled, by people casually strolling through a garden, and the snake was attempting to get away, the man said, by shedding his skin until he'd run out of skin.

"What is this garden?" she asked the man, turning away from the misery of the snake. His passion?

The man was silent.

"Are we in Eden?" she pressed him.

He only looked at her.

"Gethsemane?"

He only looked at her as if disappointed in her. Then he asked:

"Have you forgotten about Dan? Have you lost consciousness of the Rainbow Serpent? Damballah? Aido Hwedo? Who wrapped his body around the Earth to create a globe?"

The strollers moved across the plane of her dream, and the snake looked into the dreamer's eyes with a mournful stare, his body translucent, all color gone; you could count his bones.

Tongue hanging by a thread.

She looked closely and saw markings, foreign to her, etched on the dangling tongue, suddenly disembodied.

○ ⦵ ○ repeated and repeated.

She thought she woke in tears.

Then, as is usual with dreamtime, she was somewhere else. A larger, more orderly garden, everything tagged by its Latin name—Kew?—which as soon as she apprehended it became a city street, gray buildings blocking out light, drizzle falling. Ladies in long white dresses carried parasols, purple sashes with gold letters were draped across their bodices. Parasols, not umbrellas.

The snake reappeared.

The sashed women skipped over it like fearless school-girls.

When she finally woke, she lay in bed for a long time, pondering her dream. She carried it with her through the first pipe of the day, and the first cup of coffee, cut with chicory, so strong and so bitter it propelled itself down her throat, or seemed to. The burning woke her further.

She remembered the sashed women from a recent newspaper article where the gold letters spelled out VOTES FOR WOMEN. She could not recall what words were spun across the women in her dream.

Suffragettes in a formal garden, where specimens were collected, staked, labeled. Everything orderly, but the suffering snake.

The article had described force-feeding, the torture of ladylike purple-and-gold-sashed Englishwomen, and in her dream she had transformed them into schoolgirls, skipping through the imperial collection. She wasn't being fair.

She focused on the snake.

Some people could do so much damage and never take notice. Not notice the killing of a snake, or, if they did, consider it a nuisance well rid of, forcing itself to skin itself alive.

Snakes were everywhere in her landscape. She tried not to pay them any mind. But she half expected to come out one morning, greet her bottle trees, and find each wrapped in an embrace.

Have you forgotten about Dan? Have you lost consciousness of the Rainbow Serpent? Damballah? Aido Hwedo? Who wrapped his body around the Earth to create a globe?

She had not the faintest notion what ∘ ⚵ ∘ signified, yet it lived in her brain.

Have you forgotten the cacique who asked the Spanish, as they tied him to a stake and implored him to accept Christ as his savior before they set him afire, if there were people like them in Heaven? And when they assured him *yes,* said, "I'd rather go to Hell. Do what you must."

That she'd not forgotten. One of her favorite tales dangling from her mother's family tree. Thinking of it now, she realized again that there had been a spark amidst the befuddlement, in the crazy quilt of a mother she'd had.

The river crawled with snakes. And snakebirds. Reptilian necks suddenly rising above the water, achieving flight.

And her hair snaked with the least encouragement.

All of a sudden a cottonmouth—curled around her eggs in a half-submerged rotting log—moved, making her presence felt, a delicate ripple barely disturbing the surface of the water, her white mouth, soft and open, yawning into its darkness.

When her hair snaked, her mother said it was going back to Africa.

"Look like you going home, pickney," she said. And the swashbucklers and petty nobility fell away. Then: "Tell no one I said that, *ma fille,*" speaking out of her *gens inconnu* mouth.

If you didn't know the river, its environs, the snakebird could fool you.

One chair, Annie's, was all the furniture on the porch, which looked out on snakes and snakebirds and took comfort in the ancient properties of bottle trees. Her Kongolese charm, Mary Ellen Pleasant had said, assuring her also that this fear of snakes was not right, was imposed over a natural, and ancient, alliance.

"In Africa snakes are worshiped. And I don't mean

some crass snake charmer in the village square. No. Snakes are worshiped as actors in the prime cause: avatars, cousins of the prime mover."

M.E.P. said it was obvious to her: Western, European, civilization, so-called, depended on the need for enemies. "Look around," she said. "All you have to do is look around."

"When one enemy falls, they create another. It helps them pass the time."

"Africans waged war," Annie suggested.

"Of course they did," M.E.P. agreed, "but not a chance against the European system, or should I say onslaught?"

"Tell me who you are," M.E.P. asked her at supper that night in 1858, following on Mrs. Harper and the Tremont Temple. They were not supping at Mrs. Pleasant's establishment of choice; Annie's costume would not permit entry. She looked as close as could be to a man, not a dandy, more like a mule driver.

"Someone interested in the race."

"That is obvious from your remarks to the speaker. What else? Where do you come from?"

"I was born on an island in the Caribbean. I left there awhile ago. My family remains."

"Slave or free?"

"A bit of both."

"And what occupies you here?"

"Boston?"

"Boston, America; wherever."

"I recognize your name."

"Do you recall from where?"

"We may have friends in common."

"That would be nice." M.E.P. smiled, nodding to the waiter about to deposit food and drink in front of them on the newspaper-covered table. They were in the back room of a restaurant by the waterfront, owned by a Negro fisherman and his wife. They treaded lightly and so far had not had their boat burned. "You are very young."

"Nearly twenty."

"That is very young."

"You come of age early in the tropics."

"Negroes have to come of age early, of necessity."

"Yes."

"Part of our struggle is to give our children childhood."

It was soon after that meeting, after several evenings spent with M.E.P. and others, over fish stew in the back room of the Free Enterprise, as the restaurant was called, that Annie discarded her Christian, given name, which M.E.P. said sounded too much like the royal orifice, and became Annie Christmas, whose life story, legend, M.E.P. recounted to her.

"It's all well and good to dress as a man in the cause, my dear, but for heaven's sake, take a *nom de guerre* fit for a woman."

Annie smiled, hearing her mother's voice in the tone, if not the words. Listen, *ma fille.*

"My dear," M.E.P. went on, "*there* was a woman to conjure with."

"Tell me."

"A fine figure of a woman, as they say. And then some. Six feet, eight inches tall, weighing two hundred pounds. You may have her name."

"Is it yours to give?"

"Inasmuch as your taking it is a way to keep the name alive, unforgotten."

"Tell me about her."

"She worked the river, the Mississippi, and when she kissed its waters in gratitude for her livelihood, she drained the river fourteen miles in each direction. She once towed a keelboat, a great flat-bottomed boat, from New Orleans to Natchez at a full run. No one would have dared slap any chains on her, believe you me."

"When was she supposed to have lived?"

"She lived around revolutionary times.

"As I was saying, she was quite a woman. Occasionally she got all dressed up and put on her thirty-foot-long necklace, on which each bead signified eyes, noses, and ears she had gouged out or bitten off in fights."

"I imagined the beads were to count each year of her life."

"You are too sensible. Although she'd done considerable damage in her fights, she herself was intact. In fact, . . ."

"Fact?"

"Fact. As much as anything is fact. She was very beautiful, drawing the stares of men as well as women. She was seen floating on her barge seated on a crimson chair, drinking champagne from a solid silver goblet, poured by her high yaller maid . . ."

"Careful. Remember who I am underneath all this."

"You are who you are underneath all that. Skin is beside the point."

"How did she die? Or didn't she?"

"Peacefully. And when she died her twelve sons put her body on her barge, and all thirteen of them drifted down the river and out to the Caribbean and were never seen again. She was, of course, African—born there, I mean."

"Of course. And imaginary."

"Why can't you allow yourself to believe in her?"

"Because she's unbelievable."

"If so many can believe in that other twelve and their divine center, water into wine, rolling back the stone, rising up, take-up-thy-bed-and-walk, Lazarus, why can't you believe in her?"

"It's too much; that's all."

"A messianic sister with the physical power of John Henry; too much to hope for, maybe."

"Maybe."

"Is Nanny too much?" M.E.P. named the great Maroon chieftainess, as she was known, also conjurer, obeah-woman, science-woman, physician, warrior, herself with a necklace, signifying her life, one made from the teeth of white men. Her women followers were bedecked likewise, teeth around their wrists and ankles.

"You know of her?"

"Her renown has traveled far."

"I don't know that I can believe all the stories I learned about her."

"Who told you about her? Your mother?"

"God, no. A woman named Industry; she was my nurse."

"And what did she tell you?"

"She slept on a pallet next to my bed, on the floor. She would sit there at night, beside me, after I had said my prayers, and, if as antidote to them, would spin the tales of Nanny and her Windward Maroons. All her magic, all her fierceness. I was a child, and I believed in her. In my mind I fixed Industry and Nanny as somehow one and the same. Maybe she told the stories in the first person; I don't recall. When Industry ran off I knew she had turned back into her Nanny-self. I hoped so."

"Well then, who's to say that's not the case?"

"I was a child."

"Where do you have trouble? At the cauldron seething with the bodies of Red Coats, water so hot their brass buttons have clarified into their original elements? Or at Nantucompong . . . ?"

"How do you know that word?"

"Oh, we have Maroons here too, you know."

"Were any able to catch a bullet between their buttocks and fire it back?"

"They say Nanny taught them to use their hands in that way. They could catch bullets barehanded and fire them back. She kept the magic of her buttocks and breasts too, for herself alone."

"You believe this?"

"Do the magic pumpkin seeds stop you? Or the fact that if a white man crosses her grave he dies instantly? Which stops you?"

"I grew up, was conceived and raised, in the realm of fantasy. I have little, if any, use for it."

"For some, this is fantasy; for others, history."

"Yes, perhaps."

"No perhaps. You believed in Industry. That she and Nanny were one. That she descended from Nanny."

"I was a child. And I wanted her to get away."

"Who knows? Maybe she took to the hills to wage the war of the flea."

"No. They caught her. She was brought back. They put her in the stocks by the sugar mill. Punishment for what they called her 'contumacious conduct.' When Industry cursed them, they put the bit on her.

"Bear in mind that this was after emancipation, after the slaves of the empire were freed. After 'Jubilee, Jubilee, this year of Jubilee, when Queen Victoria set we free.' But things lingered on. As they probably will here.

"Anyway, Industry was eventually released from the stocks. But when I left, seven years later, she was still wearing the bit. Still eating rust. In silence."

"And there was nothing you could do to save her."

"That's right. I couldn't save her. I saved myself instead."

．　　．　　．

"Think about it. What if one or all of Annie's sons made landfall on your island? Can you conjure yourself as descending from him, them, and, therefore, her?"

"I am here to leave that place behind me."

"That you will never do. Never. Take the name. Maybe it will make a believer out of you."

So she took the name, and used it and when she withdrew, she withdrew to the original Annie's bailiwick, almost without thinking.

On her riverbank, she was surrounded by silence, except for the occasional serenade from the bottle trees, the now and then blast of a riverboat, the bleat of the *anhinga*, or the interruption of white boys, armed with fishing poles or shotguns, yelling "Old Spook" toward her dwelling, enshrouded by river fog, masked by moss and trees.

Whatever did they make of the bottle trees? she wondered. Probably thought she was a drunkard. A moonshiner hanging her vessels out to dry.

Or a witch. She figured an old cinnamon-colored, white-haired woman scared them a hell of a lot more than they scared her.

Their greeting, usually in the early morning or at twilight, depending on the nature of their game, was not her only contact with them.

She sometimes watched them pass by in silence, shrouded all in white, spotless, sheets ironed only as a wife can iron, their shoes caked with the mud of the Mississippi riverbank.

Torches lighting the insignia on some of their breasts, signifiers of rank.

Those times they did not call out to her. She was beside the point, by the way.

Their presence was not her only contact with other living humans.

For that she walked north to Carville.

II.

Plague

U.S. Public Health Service Station #66

Leprosy is a disease peculiar to humans.

Like many diseases to which the word *plague* is applied, leprosy carried (carries) with it a sense of retribution, payback.

Carriers belong in the Ninth Circle.

No one knows exactly how, or when, leprosy entered the United States.

It is safe to guess that the disease flourishes among the darker races.

When you read the literature on leprosy, also known as Hansen's disease, the search for point of entry into the U.S.A. appears as crucial as the search for cure, vaccine.

It is a problem of biblical proportions.

Theories abound.

Okay. Everyone seems to agree that the disease was

brought here by someone deliberately, someone out to settle a score, to contaminate the United States. Among those prominently cited are Africans and Acadians. A coffle of slaves from a seasoning station in the Caribbean, whose tropical moisture is a hothouse for the bacteria that causes the affliction. Exiled Acadians from *les provinces maritimes;* let the good times roll.

Let us take a hypothetical case:

What if a slave, from Jamaica, Cuba, Surinam, Brazil, Barbados, the Virgins, any of the Lesser or Greater Antilles, emerges from the water, a man in an iron mask, the scourge spreading to his extremities. He is belled around the neck. What if he finds a way to propel himself across the water; what if he sets out to discover America?

What if he is armed only with his disease? These are dangerous times; it is every man for himself.

He is everyman, of a sort.

For comfort he has only a pouch of tobacco, a bottle of rum, some cornbread wrapped in a square of kente cloth.

But he must remain uncomforted; the iron mask stands between him and food, smoke, and drink. He puts each against the iron, and sniffs as best he can through the sieve under his nose, five punched holes. The smells of food, smoke, and drink could drive him crazy.

He sets out, the sun burning the surface of the Caribbean, burning the iron on his face, the bell around his neck, his skin is cooking behind metal, he is dying of thirst, he must find land and a blacksmith to remove the mask.

The scourge is spreading over him, silently.

The mask is locked behind his neck, the bell is secured to the mask. There is a constant ringing in his ears.

He might make music, but he can't control the sound.

This is all hypothetical, mind you.

But what if this hypothetical, hungry, thirsty, being-driven-crazy man made landfall at the mouth of the Mississippi, or washed ashore like Robinson Crusoe, or Prospero, and began walking across the landscape of the United States of America in search of a black blacksmith, leaving a trail of fingers and toes in his wake?

What if someone picks up a brown finger or an ebony toe as a memento, has the finger or toe pierced and made into an amulet he wears around his neck, or ground into a love charm which he drinks dissolved in warm water, believing in blackness, a cure for what ails him? The same kind of thing, the avidity for black bodily parts, happened at lynchings, where there was a brisk trade.

What then?

Or maybe our carrier is not a runaway, a man in an iron mask, littering the American landscape with fingers and toes until he runs out of fingers and toes. Maybe our missing link is a woman, described by the trader as "possessed of a good set of teeth; pliant in limb; free of venereal taint; dreamy-eyed; a fast breeder; her babies have flattish noses owing to a continued rubbing against her back."

She stands in the open-air market in Charleston or St. Augustine or Louisville waiting to be sold, unknowing host to the disease, potential contaminant.

.   .   .

It has been customary (*cf.* Leviticus 13:14) to associate the leprous person with uncleanness.

This has necessitated, since the time of Lazarus, and before, the setting apart of the leprous person, so as not to endanger the clean, as opposed to unclean, individual.

Colonies were founded for this purpose.

Around New Orleans, in the nineteenth century, the first leper colony in the United States of America was opened, built on Metairie Ridge behind the Big Easy.

A wild, untamed place, it was covered with scrub and palmetto and overrun with scorpions. Known to all as La Terre Lepraux, terrible things happened there. The lepers ran wild, threatened to invade the city limits. They were promiscuous and bred indiscriminately.

Further enclosure, stricter colonization, was called for.

Enter the sisters of St. Vincent de Paul, who brought order out of chaos.

The order secured a place on the Mississippi, known as the Indian Camp Plantation, built on the site of a Houma Indian village. The main house was handsome, of stuccoed red brick, with Doric columns and a wide verandah.

The house became the convent.

The quarters out back, up against the remains of rice fields, suited the lepers just fine. Bobolinks sang welcome.

Getting the lepers there from La Terre Lepraux was something else again.

The riverboats refused to carry the diseased, even when the nuns pleaded with them, invoking Christian charity.

A solution was eventually reached, and the lepers were transported to their new home under cover of darkness, on abandoned coal barges steered by convicts from the House of Detention on Tulane Avenue. After the transportation was completed, the barges were set afire on the river, the residue of coal dust sparking way up into the night sky, showering the live oak and cypress trees, hissing into silence on their descent into the waters.

Things between the lepers and the outside world mellowed over time, now that everyone was out of harm's way. It became customary for the Mississippi riverboats to salute the lepers with three long blasts from their whistles as they passed the old plantation, on the banks of the river.

Gamblers laid down their hands and tipped their wide-brimmed hats in the direction of the lepers.

After the nuns died off, or were sent on, the place was taken over by the United States government, whose Public Health Service runs it today.

At Carville, Annie Christmas entered the grounds through a tear in the wire fence, through which two lepers had once run off to get married.

No intramural marriages were allowed.

From the tear in the fence she passed by the graveyard, the lines of headstones, plain, with a number where a name would be in the ordinary world.

Everyone was numbered.

Numbers were sewn into garments, etched into cots, called out by nurses.

Is it any wonder Bingo! was the favorite pastime of many of the inmates?

Except for this numericalization of individuals, and a few other details, every effort had been made to replicate the original, the ordinary world they had left outside.

But the world most of them had known was of another century.

The colony became a pastiche of the twentieth under the auspisces of the U.S.P.H.S.

The Public Health Service opened a movie house, with the latest silents shipped from the Pathé Company in New York City, part of a charitable arrangement, and tax-deductible. Serials. Comedies. Westerns. William S. Hart. The Keystone Kops. And high drama, like *The Birth of a Nation*, which received a curious reception.

Leprosy, the reverend mother had explained to Annie when she first petitioned for visiting privileges, flourished among the darker races. Indeed, the lepers hailed from all over the non-Western world. They came from the Caribbean, the American West (one man had ridden with Red Cloud; one woman had danced the Ghost Dance), the Sea Islands, as well as Hawai'i, the Philippines, and the northern coast of South America (a Sephardic Maroon from the Surinam jungle, for one), and Africa.

"It is like writing history with lightning," President Wilson declared, arranging showings of Griffith's twelve-reeler to Congress and the Supreme Court.

Its effects were far-reaching. One citizen, a man
named William J. Simmons, a former member of the Wood-
men of the World, saw *The Birth* and found himself longing
for an organization to call his own. On Thanksgiving 1915,
he gathered some friends on top of Stone Mountain,
Georgia. They burned a cross. He christened them the
Invisible Empire.

Mr. Simmons gazed into the blackened white men
pounding their shoes on congressional tables, aping the
likes of John Mercer Langston and Hiram J. Revels. So did
the Saturday night audience at the colony.

Their response was different.

They rose in silence and filed out into the warm
Louisiana night.

They did not speak back to the screen in their native
languages, as they did in comedies, serials, westerns.

They walked out and refused to return.

With a nod to their disobedience, the authorities arranged with the Pathé Company to ship south some of the
movies made by Oscar Micheaux. *The Virgin of the Semi-
nole, Homesteader,* and *Veiled Aristocrats* were greatly ap-
preciated.

In addition to the movies there was a nine-hole miniature golf course, with obstacles like a wishing well,
Rheinish castle, network of trenches based on the Western Front. There were tennis courts and a bowling alley
with duck pins. Those with finger and toe drops kept
score.

There was a soda fountain, where lepers jerked sodas

and scooped ice cream and split bananas, and where the unreal red of maraschino cherries reflected in the stainless steel of the fountain.

There were gardens dating back to antebellum days, like the original architecture, providing continuity. They sported roses and lilacs and long arcades of purple wisteria, and you could almost see the ladies in big fat dresses strolling arm in arm, reciting poetry, talking war news, where lepers now turned the earth and laid down mulch to protect the ancient plantings. Once a leper turned up a pearl earring, encrusted with dirt and rotted leaves, and he was unaccountably moved at his discovery.

Socials were held once a week in the gymnasium. Dancing was encouraged; sex was not. One leper blew a hot clarinet. In the original, ordinary world he would have given Sidney Bechet a run for his money. "My daddy rocks me with a heavy roll." The joint was jumping.

A woman beat out rhythms Annie recalled from girl-hood, with most of one hand missing.

She loved these people, once she found them, hidden away as she had hidden herself. Many from her part of the world.

They had not always been leprous.

They spoke of families, mothers, fathers, lovers, friends—with whom contact was forbidden, on each side.

They wondered if their names were called at holiday gatherings. When candles were lit; noisemakers rattled; wishbones split.

Annie shared in their wonder: When the suckling pig

is buried in red-hot coals on Christmas morning, and the rum punch is being poured, is my name called? Does anyone say: "I wonder what ever happened . . . ?"

In the colony, new kinship was forged.

Oral History

Some passed up miniature golf, tennis, Bingo!; others, after a few tries, found these distractions tiresome, and lacked the dexterity or interest to sustain a game.

For these story-telling became the main pastime, and, once discovered, was never relinquished.

Stories of the original, outside world, and their place in it, were passed from mouth to mouth.

Stories of the days in La Terre Lepraux, safeguarded by some of the old-timers among them, were released.

Oral histories of lepers breaking out of the landscape, and into the City, terrorizing innocent people; lepers looting stores, leaving behind notes: "This is the hand of a leper"; lepers disrupting the auction block—mainstay of the city's commerce—jumping onto the platform and kissing the auctioneer, appalling the paying customers.

No wonder the authorities were forced to enclose them. They threatened the common good. They were outrageous, anarchic.

"Wonderfully so," said the speaker.

Some among them had a burning desire to escape. Some did not. Some had made their peace with the place, and their affliction; others not so. There were stories about a flatboat tied and hidden among the reeds at the riverside. There were stories of one man in particular, labeled incorrigible, trying to make his way back to Hawai'i, where his people were.

He descended from feathered kings, so he said, and carried with him a long thigh bone as an amulet, on which was scrimshawed the last moments of Captain Cook, the work of the Hawai'ian's great-grandfather, a gift to his great-grandson, who in turn is telling the tale of the scrimshaw to some of his fellow lepers, in his great-grandfather's words, one humid Saturday night as the rest of the colony watches a tennis tournament under newly installed lights.

"When we first laid eyes on them they were sitting on the beach—and I don't intend this as an apology—I want to tell you what happened.

"They were sitting on the beach. Their longboats, plain of decoration, unlike our own canoes—or those of the Maori, Mayan, Arawak, Carib, Aztec, Ashanti, Yoruba, Samoan, Inuit—all the people we met on the seas—their longboats were pulled up against the shore, which they called, we found out later, the Strand. This comforted them, it seemed, and satisfied their desire to christen everything anew—even us.

"On the day of the first sighting we were at a distance, but we could see them clearly. Their clothes were as plain as their boats. And heavy. It was as if they hadn't planned on ending up here, under our blazing sun. As if, as they made their progress across the world, the sun would be the one they knew from home. Their own sun would follow them, light their way, make them comfortable.

"Each of them had a thick piece of red flesh in his hands; red juice ran down each chin, matting their beards, attracting sandflies. We thought they were chewing on an enemy, celebrating as we might.

"Our mistake. They were merely refreshing themselves and cooling off, with watermelon they'd taken from a garden near the shore. We later noticed a trail of smashed melons leading to the beach, as if the strangers were aghast at our bounty.

"Be that as it may, we were very relieved, and laughed. I mean, had it been what we first imagined, we might have been next. We laughed at this, and from our misunderstanding came a new way to describe watermelon: *Ka 'ai waha 'ula 'ula o ka āina*—which means in English: 'the red-mouthed food of the land.' When we told them later, over glasses of rum on board the *Discovery,* they didn't see the joke.

"They were serious men, here on serious business.

"They were devouring pieces of blood-red melon—

not the pale version they must have been used to, if they knew it at all. For watermelon demands a long, hot growing season.

"We went further in our joking—but kept it to ourselves. We called them *akua waha 'ula 'ula*—the 'red-mouthed gods.' They were no more gods than we were, but seemed unsure of that. They helped themselves to the world as if they had created it.

"At first I liked James Cook. He seemed like a fair man, a technician rather than an ideologue—at first. No aristocrat, he had been a farmboy in England, and then realized he had a gift for navigation. He found a patron and was on his way. In more ways than one.

"The end began in his misapprehension. A few of the younger men took a longboat from the side of the *Discovery*. Their intention was to decorate the boat with carving, commemorating Cook's visit to the islands. In so doing we would celebrate his departure, for which by this time we were eager; at the same time we would honor him. It is our custom, as you know, to give a gift, a memento, to see someone on his way, as I give this thigh bone to you on the occasion of your first voyage.

"We were eager for his departure. Too many liberties taken, for one thing. We could sense what was coming. We wanted to avoid bloodshed, which bloodshed was becoming inevitable with our growing realization that these Englishmen did not simply wish to visit us, to 'discover' us, as they put it. They wanted to own us, and the islands, tame the landscape to their purposes, tame even the slopes of

Kilauea. Now what would Pele have done about that? We had to save them from themselves, and us from them.

"So we decided to send them on their way, in celebration, with feasting, and let the Maori take care of them.

"They had no respect for wildness; they wanted to bring everything to order.

"So we took the longboat, and when Cook found out it was missing something in him snapped. He went wild. Truly. He set out with an armed party for shore. Captured some of our people on the way to me. He arrived finally and demanded my arrest, and punishment by flogging, like a common sailor, for the missing boat. Well, you can imagine what transpired.

"All hell, as they say, broke loose. The anger of the people, which I and a few others had managed to keep at a simmer, exploded. We sought Pele. She, in response, sent a trickle from her core, red-hot, burning. We thanked her with an offering of green-lipped mussels, a favorite of the sharp-lipped goddess.

"With her divine blessing the people set upon Cook and his men, driving the landing party back to the sea, but encircling Cook on the shore. Saving, and savoring him for themselves. His men, on the high seas on their way to the *Discovery*, barely looked back.

"This bone tells the story; see for yourself."

The great-grandfather's voice was silent. The great-grandson spoke now in his own words.

"We all know how history comes down to us, which

stories, which versions tend to be passed on. What my great-grandfather told me, what he carved into this bone, was the heroic version, the one he wanted to become history. But the real story is not as colorful, not as tidy; it never is.

"James Cook made a serious mistake. He returned to us. The journey on which he lost his life was his second journey to Hawai'i, which, in homage to his patron, he had christened the Sandwich Islands. You might well laugh, given our reputation, well earned, for anthropophagy.

"On his first journey all seemed well. His arrival was celebrated traditionally, with feasting and the exchange of gifts. We sent him on his way with good cheer, even as the syphilis was beginning to work its way into the bloodstream of our people, and the bones, and the brain. We had been syphilized, my friends, cured of our savage state.

"His murder, and he was most definitely murdered, was retribution for this, as much as for other matters.

"When he returned, the people were waiting for him. Each night the air was filled with war chants, invoking Pele. God only knows what they made of the serenade on Cook's ship. In the day, the chants, the drumming, continued, unrelenting. And a red-hot trickle ran from Pele's core.

"The longboat *was* taken, more to provoke Cook into giving chase than for any other reason, the last in a series of thefts. An hourglass was stolen by the only Hawai'ian in Cook's crew, a cabin boy purloined on an earlier voyage. The boy tied the glass inside his blouse and swam home. But before he escaped, the boy let others on board, and a sextant, spyglass, and a cask of rum came up missing. The longboat was the last straw.

"The people knew they could count on Cook's response to the theft. On his voyage south with the captain the cabin boy had observed behavior that became increasingly bizarre. But then Cook's own syphilis was in a late stage. The ship's doctor, the cabin boy reported, wondered if the captain had succumbed to calenture, the rapture of warm waters, which could send a European off his head. Or if, witnessing some of his crew as long pig had rattled him. That he was syphilitic was denied until much later.

"Upon discovering the longboat missing, Cook went wild, as my great-grandfather reported. He came ashore and ordered my great-grandfather arrested and flogged. He declared himself the king maker of the Hawai'ians. Poor devil. The people chased him, cornered him on the beach, pursued him up the rock face behind it, and out onto a ledge, where the people pulled him limb from limb, tossing the head, eyes ice blue, Antarctic, down the rock face, bouncing into the harbor where the *Discovery* was at anchor. The people built a fire on the rock face, and the captain's flesh was roasted, and the captain's bones were cooled and distributed as war souvenirs.

"But, my gods, I doubt they would have eaten him, a white man in the third stage of syphilis. Then again, maybe they did.

"I must take my great-grandfather's words that this is Cook's actual femur, even though on close inspection I detect no deterioration from the disease, but the scrimshaw probably would mask that sort of thing. So who's to say? It makes for an interesting conversation piece, like Cook's skull, retrieved from the harbor floor by the same cabin boy, seated above his grandmother's cookstove on a shelf. She uses it to keep onions.

"Note, if you will, my great-grandfather's omissions. The contamination of the people by venereal disease has not been inscribed. He has, in his words, as I remember them, and in the images he has carved in the bone, purified the experience. He has made a monument. To our people's innocence. Never suggesting that the women and some of the men went along with the English sailors willingly, for payment of biscuits or rum or belladonna.

"The truth, I suspect, lies somewhere in between. It usually does."

> Dip dem, Bedward, dip dem,
> Dip dem in de healing stream.
> Dip dem deep, but not too deep,
> Dip dem fe cure bad feeling.

Annie was in fine voice this afternoon, serenading a group of lepers as they bathed in the shallows of the Mississippi, clouds of silt raised underwater, lit by the sunlight glancing into the river. Brown clouds rising and falling, settling, rising again.

Annie was propped against the exposed root of a live oak tree, one foot bent back against the riverbank; she looked like a great waterbird, a stork, or heron. Her head held back in song, haloed in white. Her cinnamon skin shone in the sunlight. One slender arm gestured as her voice took on the twang of her native land.

Her song was by way of introduction to her story, for it was her turn this afternoon.

"It is my belief," Annie began, "that the history of my people, the history of my part of the world, is of the one-step-forward, two-step-back variety. I realize that's not confined to my part of the world. I am by nature, as you know, a historical pessimist. But it seems to me . . . oh, let me get on with the story of Bedward for you; then perhaps my feelings will be made clear.

"Alexander Bedward was a healer, prophet, asylum inmate, early Pan-Africanist, flying African manqué. Bedward was baptized into the Jamaica Native Baptist Church by one H.E.S. Woods, a man everyone knew better as Shakespeare II. True-true.

"Shakespeare II was a founding father of the Jamaica Native Baptist Church and a prophet in his own right. He saw in Bedward great things; while still a child Alexander was chosen to play Ariel in Shakespeare II's version of *The Tempest,* performed annually, always out of doors, and always during hurricane season. Shakespeare II held a special prayer service begging Massa God to send high winds and heavy rains. No wonder they called him a madman. And thought he passed his madness to his protégé.

"Alexander grew into a strapping man, and into the role of Caliban, of course, which Shakespeare II cast in the mold of Toussaint, for audiences who had never heard of Toussaint but had been taught about Caliban in school.

"This all took place in August Town, a town named for the date of manumission. August first, 1834. Actually, manumission occurred on August first, 1838, since former slaves were required to serve a four-year apprenticeship-to-freedom before full emancipation was granted. Some—myself and Shakespeare II included—believe it never was.

"The healing stream into which Bedward immersed his followers was the Hope River, named for Major Richard Hope, one of the original founders of Jamaica, owner of Hope Sugar Estate, namesake of Hope Gardens, where even as I speak, peacocks stroll through a maze modeled after the one at Hampton Court.

"The most important tributary of the Hope River was the Mammee, the Akan word for mother. Names are extremely important," she said softly, and her enumerated friends nodded. "They tell us so much."

"The source of the healing stream and the Mammee was in the Blue Mountains, near the site of Nanny Town. You remember Nanny; I have spoken of her time and again."

"Yes, indeed," one of the company answered for the rest.

"The source is to be found in the cascade of water which washes the mountains, near where a flock of white birds, the souls of Nanny and her soldiers, gathers each evening at dusk. Near where the faces of Nanny and her soldiers are imprinted in the trunks of lignum vitae.

"But back to Bedward. He was actually a nationalist in priest's vestments, trained and inspired by Shakespeare II. He particularly rattled the colonial authorities intent on order, terrified should the masses become uncontrollable, and the aisles of cane strangled by escaped native growth, sending the colony into ruination. When Bedward prophesied that 'the black wall shall crush the white wall' in his best Calibanesque voice, the authorities realized this was not a homily of architecture, and its speaker not some country parson who dabbled in community theater, and Bedward was locked away as a madman.

"He is usually remembered as a madman. One who gathered his flock from all over the island and disappointed them in his promise to spin around, rise, and fly back to Africa. One step forward, two steps back. Ah, me.

"He remains in the asylum today. Likewise will happen to Marcus Mosiah Garvey. You mark my words."

"And Shakespeare II?" someone asked.

"He jumped to his death, all got up like Titus Andronicus."

"The perfect name, we thought. Not without irony."

A Tahitian, newly arrived at Carville, was being welcomed into the story-telling group.

"Mr. Christian, that is. What a laugh.

"You need to know the reason for the journey in the first place. In Tahiti, Bligh had loaded the ship with breadfruit trees, which he was accused of pampering, and did, watching over them like a mother hen. Giving the sailors' water rations to the seedlings, for example.

"You have probably heard that part of the story. The sadistic captain, too quick with the cat, favoring a tree over his own men."

A few in the group nodded.

"But those trees were not for show. They were a vital investment. They were necessary to save an even more vital adventure in capital. The sugar industry.

"The year of the mutiny was a time of panic among the planters of the Caribbean, and in turn the merchants who purveyed their goods. Hurricanes had decimated the grounds where the slave diet was cultivated. The American war had brought a blockade against the islands, stopping any goods passing between the English possessions and the American mainland. No salted cod from Boston, for example, another staple of the slave diet. For the time being the Triangle lost one of its points. Things looked desperate.

"Slaves, the dearest investment of all, were beginning to starve. And then the word came down that a magical tree lived in the South Seas, and it grew bread! Imagine!"

"I remember it well," Annie Christmas said. "Bligh was dispatched under orders of the crown and the Jamaica Assembly to import the breadfruit. In fact, he had much to do with the botanical rearranging of the island. Not only did he bring the magical breadfruit tree. He brought the Jew plum—no, Rachel," Annie caught the eye of one of the company, "I have no idea why . . . sorry. And the otaheite apple.

"But then the island was in an almost constant state of reordering. Ganja came with the coolies in 1845, ackee with slaves from the Bight of Benin, banana from the Canary Islands with the Spanish in 1520.

"And then there was Lord Rodney's ship the *Flora*, aptly named, an apotheosis of importation. She carried into our midst nutmeg, cinnamon, mango, for example. Coffee from Ethiopia. Aloe, the only plant brought out of Eden, from southern Africa. And on and on and on.

"They never could let well enough alone. Not when there's a profit to turn, a conquest to be made. The same syllogism to prove: that man is superior, and that white man is supreme. The empiricism of empire. The imbalancing of the world. The mongoose from India is brought to the Caribbean to control the wildlife of the canefields. God save us from wildlife, wild life. The mongoose eats everything in its path, save the Africans cutting cane. I really didn't mean to go on so. Please . . ."

"*Rien de tout*," the Tahitian acknowledged Annie, then returned to her story.

"I am pleased that you raise slavery, for slavery figures further in the history of the mutineers. Fletcher Christian and his men, it is said, populated their island colony by taking Tahitian women as their, so to speak, wives. Much is made in this version of bare breasts. The pale Englishman in thrall to the brown tits of Polynesia. We become fetish, drive them mad. They collect us in the flesh, on postage stamps, in their museums.

"What is not said, never, as far as I can tell, is that these women had husbands already, and in some cases children by their Tahitian men. But, just like that, Christian and his cohorts enslaved the Tahitian men. At gunpoint, of course. It was astonishing how easily these sailors were transformed into the lords of all they surveyed. How languidly they went about their new life.

"Time went by. The slave men saw their wives impregnated. The women were told to give the slave men, their husbands, orders. To watch as one recalcitrant man was whipped by Christian, as effortlessly as Bligh ever wielded punishment, I daresay. And one warm Pacific night, the palm trees rustling, the blossoms of the sacred otaheite dropping to the ground, the trade winds coming up, the slave men rose as the moon rose, and sliced Mr. Christian's throat across, and some other throats, and set themselves free, stealing a boat and rowing back across the open sea to their original island, and the children they left behind. To their backs were the women, the remaining white men, and the mongrel children. Where they are today, in one form or another. Where they speak a language caught in time.

"When the *Topaz*, a Yankee clipper out of Boston, engaged in the China trade, was blown off course and came upon Pitcairn and the remnant of mutineers and their motley colony, no one revealed the real story. The captain was told only that these men—there couldn't have been more than three or four left—survived a shipwreck and stumbled on paradise; nothing could make them leave. They only asked that they might barter several dozen coconuts for a chest of China tea. The captain agreed, distributing the taste of paradise, as he called the coconuts, to his crew lined up on the beach. The men pierced the fruit, lifted it to their lips, tilted their heads back, and drank the white milk from the brown and hairy tit.

"The men of the *Topaz* returned to Boston, where there was speculation that they had encountered the survivors of the mutiny. If so, the captain wondered, who was Mr. Christian?

"And, yes, I do realize this is the twentieth year of the twentieth century, but I want to set the record straight before the millennium."

Annie thanked the Tahitian on behalf of the company, not remarking on the mongrel status she herself owned. The woman was bitter; give her that.

Rachel DeSouza, #11246, was sitting with the circle against an arcade of wisteria, blooming, the bunches of purple flowers hanging around them.

"We remind me of one of those paintings of Greek philosophers. You know, sitting around pondering the meaning of life. Especially with this arcade behind us, our own *stoae*."

Annie smiled. "Indeed."

"Life is life," said Rachel. "It begins and it ends. Do you think that if more people believed that, that there is no great eye in the sky, no green pastures behind the clouds, do you think they would behave better?"

"Live and let live? We have not had the luxury of finding out."

"It should not be considered a luxury."

"You know that and I know that, and look where it's got us. Sitting under the wisteria in a leper colony, telling stories, like a poor man's Decameron."

"You don't really believe that."

"Sometimes," Annie said, "too much of the time, I

think all we have are these stories, and they are endangered. In years to come, will anyone have heard them—our voices?"

"Once something is spoken," Rachel said, "it is carried on the air; it does not die. It, our words, escape into the cosmos, space."

"I want to be heard here and now, on the planet Earth, not falling on deaf ears on the moons of Jupiter."

"We are doing what we can. All we can at the moment."

"Who will take responsibility for these stories?"

"We all do, Annie. It's the only way."

"See you on Saturn."

"I, Rachel DeSouza, am sending this story into the ether, on a Sunday afternoon, 1920, from the banks of the Mississippi River. I have told it before, but if space is infinite a little repetition can't hurt.

"Our floor was covered with sand. The floor of our temple. Even though we were hidden in the jungle. The Jodensavanne it was called. My last memory of that place, which I loved but had to leave—what's new? My last memory as I turned to look back, not afraid this time of becoming salt, but maybe sugar, is of the *mikva*, as the forest was surrounding it, with a greenness so deep, so thick, so determined, I thought I could detect its movement.

"When we were in Spain, under the Inquisition, during the reign of Torquemada, we worshiped in hidden rooms, some underground, some at the ends of tunnels at the backs of houses. We worshiped in secret to save our lives, and used sand on the floor to muffle the sounds of the services. Sound waves again. A wooden or tile floor and we would have been sitting ducks. But the sand quelled the sound, and we carried this tradition with us into the New World. Some people think we needed a reminder of our exile in the desert. Others think, first came the tropics, then the sand. Not at all. It was a survival tactic, as usual.

"Soon enough we had to leave Spain, under decree from Los Reyes Católicos, and as Colón set out at the behest of the same pair, so did we, and the harbor at Cádiz was clotted with ships and boats filled to the brim with Jews. Ships and boats that went every which way. Some getting no farther than Gibraltar, Morocco if they were lucky. Others, more seaworthy, more intrepid, in a convoy, following at a discreet distance behind the *Niña*, *Pinta*, and *Santa María*, in search of a new world, but for different reasons than the Admiral of the Ocean Sea, El Señor Colonización, as some of us called him.

"They crossed in late summer, the time of sudden storms. Imagine the procession of little ships, coming along behind, some in terror, seasick, homesick, caught in the inexorable currents of the Atlantic. Of course, I want to know how many went down, how many survived; where did the survivors make landfall?

"That ocean floor must be something else again. Where the sand covers centuries.

"I wonder if Don Cristóbal knew he was being followed. He probably never looked back, so intent was he on India, China. So intent he convinced himself Cuba was Japan, and took some Arawak captive to find the Great Khan. He needed them to translate from the Japanese.

"He died disillusioned, disoriented by all accounts.

"But, my God, I've gone way beyond my story. And I see my time is almost up. Suffice to say another procession of ships captured my attention and I took to the hills, a *cimarrón*."

"In my hometown, when someone was away, you know, sent to the asylum or a place like this, you said they were 'in the silence.' I'd say that sort of says it all. Maybe that's why we talk so much."

There were nods all around.

"All the more reason to keep talking," Rachel said.

The speaker was a hill woman from Kentucky, #12548, née Bethany, an exception to the general rule of darker-skinned races.

"I know I must have colored blood somewhere, else I couldn't be here, infected. Probably goes back to slavery days. Doesn't everything?

"Now, my people never had slaves, you know. Of course, if they did I probably wouldn't say. I wouldn't want you to think less of me. Sometimes I feel a little outnumbered, I'll admit that. But the fact is, they didn't own anybody.

"But they knew colored folks, that's for sure. Knew

them and traded with them. Lots did. Lots more white people and colored people did business than you'd think.

"Was a whole heap of them living in a place called Ultima Thule. That was the name someone gave this chamber in Mammoth Cave, the farthest you could get to. The Indians knew it first, called it something else. I forget. A huge room, as big as the inside of the county courthouse, but pitch black, with torches burning along the walls. When your eyes got used to it you could make out the pallets on the floor, the ashes of a cookfire, and the worldly goods of the people who lived there.

"And then the people, who were silent until we stated our purpose.

"Were five levels going down underneath the floor of the main cave. To get to Ultima Thule you had to go to the fifth level, all the way down, and then proceed way back, through an alley called Olive's Bower, where there weren't morning glories or roses or wisteria, but the rock formations were rosy enough. You walked along that passage, water trickling down each side, the occasional noise of a creature, the echo of your own sound, and came out to a river someone called the Styx, a real rushing river, miles under the earth, which had blind crawdads living in it, and eyeless fish. Honest.

"It was, is, a hell of a place. That's for sure. I can remember it like it was yesterday. My father took me both times I went. I was about eleven or twelve, I guess. I helped him carry stuff to trade with the people.

"You could say these people were 'in the silence.' I

don't think folks realize just how many settlements like this there were. Mostly in caves and swamps, both of which this country has in abundance. Unknown, but known. I don't think any official records were kept. Maybe there were songs or something. Africans mixed with Indians, Cherokee and Creek and all kinds, half-breeds, quarter-breeds, whatever. And they traded with my father and other white folks from above the ground.

"They called themselves Maroons, and they mined the caverns for lead and zinc, and came up to the surface only at night, to watch the stars and get fresh air.

"Nobody bothered them unless the state militia needed target practice, and had orders to shake them up, not let them get too comfortable. Orders to capture some slaves, round up some Cherokee for shipment out west.

"But for the most part it was peaceful between the whites and the coloreds, each kept to themselves, each was armed. Peaceful, and profitable too. Still, there was always a sense that we didn't know the kind of people we were dealing with. Anything might happen. We were careful around them. Careful on our descent into Ultima Thule, our passage through Olive's Bower, across the Styx.

"We carried our own water the ten miles down.

"I wouldn't be honest with you if I didn't say that.

"Every now and then the weekly paper ran a special issue, warning us of what the editor called the 'danger of a servile conspiracy.' He wanted to remind us, he said, that with regard to the races, we'd always live in a state of siege. It was nature, he said. And the future of the white race demanded vigilance, and was threatened by what he called complacency. It was all well and good to make a profit, but not to get too close. 'A charge to keep I have, a God to glorify,' he quoted—out of context, I might add.

"He ran articles about Gabriel Prosser, Denmark Vesey, Nat Turner; some he wrote himself, some he said he copied from those big eastern papers, like *Harper's* and *The Atlantic Monthly*. They described how these men went on a tear, a rampage. Complete with illustrations of mutilated white babies and ruined white women.

"You couldn't trust any of the darker races, the servile ones. Male or female. Indian or African. Not even those living ten feet under in Ultima Thule, surviving on blind crawdads and moonshine, mining ore, studying the constellations in secret.

"Militia came down one night, into the settlement, into Ultima Thule. They crept down the five levels, along Olive's Bower, crossed the Styx, and surprised the Maroons. The set-to that followed became legend, illustrated on the pages of the weekly. They used gunpowder to set an explosion that rocked the main chamber, firing up the pallets as the Maroons slept. Some of them managed to hide in the crevices, as they ran for their lives under cover of blackness, between the blasts of gunpowder. But most of them were either killed on the spot, or captured and killed later. The charge? Servile conspiracy to commit revolution.

"One of those tried was a man named Squire, a runaway slave from Mississippi who'd managed to make it all the way to Kentucky. He was beheaded, and his head displayed outside the county courthouse, on the town common. My mother and father took me to see it, him. His head was haloed with birds. His eyes were gone.

"My mother and father said nothing. They were 'in the silence.' As was Squire. As was I."

"How did I end up here?" Annie wondered.

"How in God's name did I end up here?"

III.

SHE WAS A FRIEND OF JOHN BROWN

Provenance

Dearest Annie,

I trust you are well and not too lonely. A body needs company, no matter how much you resist that notion. Come visit me in San Francisco when you can.

Boston, whence I am writing you, is sweltering, as is usual for this time of year. I am in the city on business, the first time I have been east since October 1859. Such a long time ago. I am much changed, as I expect you are. I wonder how you are.

I had dinner last night with a group of people at Miss Alice Hooper's. In the dreadful heat of August we were served turtle soup, sole *bonne femme*, roast beef, wild rice with brown gravy, carrots boiled to the point of death, with the Irish maid serving at the right and the black butler taking away from the left.

I was seated between two men of the cloth—one an episcopal bishop, the other a cotton mill proprietor. The conversation veered into the past, of course, to those days when righteousness and excitement came together. An almost unbeatable combination.

Miss Hooper led the way, with obvious nostalgia for that time, when ladies usually confined to Transcendental *conversazioni* in parlors where windows were concealed by heavy drapes, and the air was heavy and there was no light, when they were let loose, went roaming all over the city on war business, the work of the Sanitary Commission, etc.

You know, and I know, that it's probably a failing of mine, bred of a natural impatience and a learned mistrust, but I never had much truck with those ladies and their sewing circles. And I know that's a way of making light of their contribution to the Cause. Embroidery and abolition: threads on a runner delineating an African slave (chain stitch particularly apt), supplicating, "Am I not a woman and your sister?" I know they mean (meant) well—that phrase!!—but supplication was not our mode, and divergence was inevitable. But you know all this.

What will they think now that Boston and environs are proving attractive to southern black folks? The WAR was one thing. All that *glory!! hallelujah!!* Robert Gould Shaw (to whom everyone in Boston but the Irish claims to be related) and his dry bones mixing with African bones (for which his mother was greatly praised—eschewing Mount Auburn for a nigger trench). Think he flew back home with them? Or weighed them down? Lord, have mercy, to be responsible for them after death when all you really desire is peace and the African landscape. Promise me—should you have any say in the matter—when I die they put me all to myself?

Perhaps I am wrong. I am not much changed at all. Maybe thornier?

The occasion for dinner at Miss Alice Hooper's was an unveiling of a painting purchased on her behalf. The painting was by the Englishman Turner. A man was holding forth. He was introduced as someone or other, art critic, veteran of the war, at Antietam no less (bumped into Oliver Wendell Holmes, Jr., on the road back, someone said), sometime lecturer at Harvard, thinking of heading west to "seek his fortune." The painting as he spoke was shrouded in white, waiting for the magic moment when his description, of the artist, the critical reception (Thackeray ridiculed it, he said; that I remember), the provenance of the work, would be ended and the painting, having been shed of its shroud, might breathe.

We were sipping some fine Madeira as he spoke on, and stopped, and with a flourish drew back the white cloth and Miss Hooper's new acquisition was revealed to us, and it was something else besides.

At first it seemed a painting of a fiery sky, a stark white light was at the center, on the horizon, and a ship foundered in a stormy sea.

"What is its title?" asked someone who apparently had dozed through the introduction, or taken more than his share of the Madeira, and the claret, and the *Pouilly-Fuissé* before—Lord, these folks can drink!

Miss Hooper was graciousness itself, and spoke the

title with apparent disinterest, *"Slavers Throwing Overboard the Dead and Dying, Typhon Coming On,* painted in 1840 by Joseph Mallord William Turner, a great genius, and sympathetic to our cause." She gave sufficient information to silence the inattentive. Then she turned to me.

"Mrs. Pleasant?"

"Yes, Miss Hooper?"

"Perhaps you can instruct the company about the incident the painter was illustrating."

I wasn't at all sure. What incident had Turner chosen? Which of the hundreds that came to light? Did it coincide with those I knew?

"I'm afraid I am not at all sure."

"Oh," she said, clearly disappointed in my inability to recall, even to invent something for the guests. That awful thing that can happen at a table of invited people happened: There was dead silence. Failure lurked.

In silence we were left with the painting, which dominated the room. It might well have cast shadows across us.

I wondered who would look away first.

"Perhaps I can help, Miss Hooper," the sometime lecturer at Harvard spoke up.

"Please do, Mr. Bodley."

I finally caught his name.

There was almost a collective sigh, as words drew attention from image.

"Turner based the painting on a ship named the *Zong,* an infamous case in which the traders threw slaves, living and dead, overboard to collect the insurance money and not lose their investment."

It is with statements like those, clear and dispassion-
ate, that I am reminded of it—all of it. Who insured the
ship and its cargo? Was it Lloyd's of London, for example?
How many reputable firms? How many? How many inter-
locking directorates?

I wanted to cut off the conversation to avoid them
becoming privy to my feelings. I could feel my emotions
rising. My eyes were locked on the foreground of the
painting, where a few brown arms, some lengths of chain,
and one brown leg glanced through the waves, alongside
magnificently colored fish. The fish were clearly in their
habitat; the arms and leg and chains were alien to the sea.

I was grateful that the artist had portrayed it thus,
indicating the horror of the thing aslant, by these few
members, and a reminder of their confinement, the irons
which would take them down. It got to me, all right.

I turned to Miss Hooper. "Where will you hang it?"
I inquired.

"I have not decided yet," she responded.

Mr. Bodley, apparently eager to tell us more, spoke up.

"You know, Ruskin, whose father gave it to him as a
New Year's present in 1844, at first hung it in his home, but
eventually had to conceal it. He found it impossibly painful
to live with day after day. As I said before, it comes directly
to Miss Hooper from Ruskin himself, via a dealer, of
course."

Of course. And of course a father would give the thing
to the son to welcome the New Year. And the son would
adorn the parlor or wherever with it.

"I am sorry it caused Mr. Ruskin so much pain," I

couldn't stop myself saying, but no one seemed to catch my bitterness.

"Are there any suggestions from the assembled company?" Mr. Bodley was about to turn the question of where to hang the painting into a parlor game, with each guest trying to be cleverer than the next. At least that was my fear. You know, I really don't like to dislike people, to distrust them, but I felt the old wave wash over me (perhaps in collusion with the slaves of Turner's painting I felt about to be swept away, under) and I knew someone was about to say something to justify my distrust; why should this evening be different from so many others?

Someone did.

"The thing is behind us; surely we can enjoy the art it engendered. The man had a brilliance about him, with form, color."

I glanced at the butler, and we locked eyes briefly, noticed, we hoped, by none of them.

I turned to Miss Hooper, whose face was blanched; who remained silent.

Shortly thereafter, now deaf to all remarks, I got up, took a cigar from the humidor, causing a stir, and said good night.

I returned to the Parker House, where the doorman inquired as to what floor I was working on—this despite my evening clothes, or perhaps because of them. And I a woman of sixty! Perhaps the cigar smoke wreathing my head clouded his vision. I assured him I was a guest.

Today I head for Martha's Vineyard. I shall visit my childhood haunts, the places I grew up.

Enough of my adventures. Write me at 1661 Octavia Street, San Francisco, California, when you get the chance. If you are still among the living.

My love, as ever,
Mary Ellen

The dining room of the Parker House early the next morning was populated mostly by men of middle age, prosperous-looking, their heads bowed in conversation or in communion with their eggs. The noise of the room was dull and constant, but low. No one raised his voice. Waiters bowed slightly to take orders for the lush morning repasts people once enjoyed, all accompanied by the world-famous Parker House rolls and pots of hot coffee, the beans for which had been imported, shipped, and sold by some of the men in this very room. Pewter bowls of golden demerara adorned each table.

Behind the dark paneling the kitchen was in a frenzy, as orders piled up and the heat of the day began to rise, enhancing the glow of the ovens. One man was shaving ice over the head of another.

Back in the dining room, a man was standing—hologrammatically speaking—invisible to the unsuspecting eye—under the portrait of the autocrat of the breakfast table. The hologrammatical man wore the white waiter's jacket and black bow tie of latter-day Parker House waiters.

He was waiting on his time, when he would first be called Homeboy, then Detroit Red, then X.

When Mary Ellen Pleasant glanced in his direction, she glimpsed the shadow of someone, but that high-ceilinged, portraited, agéd room must be overwhelmed by shadows. And she was used to shadows, so he didn't frighten her. She tried to locate him in the past, not knowing he was an impression of the future. She only hoped he might offer company.

Her entry into the dining room, her request for a table, had caused a stir, and only the expression on her face, the severity of her dress, and the silver dollar in her palm stopped the headwaiter from asking with whom she was in service, on whom she was waiting.

She swept by him purposefully and chose a table to the side. She felt the eyes of the hologrammatical man over her right shoulder, felt the comfort of his breathing against her hair, as she unfolded the letter left in her pigeonhole at the desk.

"May I?" his face across from hers at the table.

"Of course," she responded without speaking.

He slid into the chair across from hers. She could see his beautiful, as yet unborn eyes before her, could see herself reflected in them.

August 5th, 1874, midnight

My dear Mrs. Pleasant,

I trust you will receive this note the first thing tomorrow morning. Patrick will be driving it to the Parker House himself.

The hour is, as I have noted, midnight. My guests have long since departed. My mother is asleep, as are the servants, and I have to myself time which is mine alone. I treasure these hours. It is now that I read, write, and exercise my mind in ways not expected of someone like myself.

No one can claim me at this moment.

I am no one's daughter; I am neither property owner nor hostess.

I am writing you because I noted your distress this evening, and your abrupt departure, and I wish to apologize for any contribution I may have made to your state of mind. I think I understand, but I cannot be entirely sure.

I was very surprised to receive the Turner painting. A well-meaning (I expect) relation arranged the purchase for me as an investment, since Turner's reputation, as is too often the case, is rising since his death.

I can only presume that this well-meaning guardian of my fortunes saw that the subject matter of the work would echo my own sentiments with regard to slavery and the trade, and make the capitalist endeavor palatable to me. I am known in my family as someone rather disdainful of investment and planning, even for a female. The responsibility of capital weighs on me. Too many New England fortunes—as you need not be reminded—rest in the enterprise of slavery, in one way or another. I have tried as much as possible to separate myself from any profit which might by any filament, however slender, have been linked to the trade.

And an interesting question of ethics arises: Did the

money, my money, paid to the art dealer on my behalf for the Turner constitute the dealer's profiting off the trade? Even at this remove?

Am I also, given the painting is an investment, guilty?

The whole thing could become a game. For if I cut every link to every enterprise which might have supported the traffic in human souls—sold every piece of stock in every maritime company, for example—I would still have to reckon with the mills, the question of property in and of itself. This is something I struggle with, believe me, and because of which I could be seen, at best, eccentric, at worst, a traitor to my class.

When I asked you at dinner about the incident the painter was illustrating, I did so with a sense of you as someone all too familiar with the horrors of slavery and the Middle Passage. Far better educated in that regard than anyone at the table, particularly poor Mr. Bodley with his extraordinary grasp of ephemera. I was prevailing on you to educate us. To be our authority. I am sorry.

I should have spoken about the *Zong*. About the white flash of typhoon at the center of the work, surely comparable, in foreboding and whiteness, to Melville's white whale and Coleridge's albatross—emblems of that belief which allowed and supported something like the slave trade. The belief which endangers the white race as well as the African. No. I should not save these thoughts for the hours I spend alone.

The thing I most regret about this past evening, and that which instigated your departure, was the remark of Bishop Cowell, which I would hope might be ascribed to overindulgence, but I am afraid not. At the moment he spoke I was stunned, and knew I could not say anything.

"Let the women keep silent in the churches, for it is not given for them to speak" ran through my brain, out of nowhere, everywhere.

There. I admit to being a coward, and so his conclusion stands without opposition.

Please accept this apology, with my respect,

Alice Hooper

I was expecting something like this. Now what? Do I respond: Dear Miss Hooper, all is forgiven? Dear Miss Hooper, would you feel better if you had no money? Dear Miss Hooper, when you contemplate the trade, can you understand the constructive use of violence in the cause of liberation? And, dear Miss Hooper, this is my final question: Can you accept, nay, believe in the deepest part of yourself, the full humanity of the African?

Dear Miss Hooper, I don't hate you and yours. I love my own.

With that the hologrammatical man, who'd been reading her mind reading the letter, smiled, and murmured, "Mary Ellen, you one hard woman."

The woman was trying.

Yes.

August 6, 1874, 9 A.M.

Dear Miss Hooper,

I hold nothing against you. I wish for you all the best. I think the difference between us may be reduced to the fact that while you focus on the background of the Turner painting, I cannot tear my eyes from the foreground. It is who we are.

Yours sincerely,
Mary Ellen Pleasant

"Out of the Cradle Endlessly Rocking"

Alice Hooper woke while it was still dark and the city silent, not realizing she had managed sleep, but at the same time certain she had dreamed, brown arms and legs on the ocean floor, drifting soundlessly down, barnacled, burnished finally by their intercourse with sand.

She shook her head awake.

The letter to Mrs. Pleasant, carefully copied onto her blue writing paper from a plain white tablet, lay on her desk to her right. She read the letter once more and, deciding it was better than nothing, but not by much, folded it carefully into a blue envelope, and wrote in her wonderfully disciplined hand across the face of it,

> *Mrs. Mary Ellen Pleasant,*
> *The Parker House.*
> > *by hand.*

Of her speechlessness she had written, Out of nowhere, everywhere.

Suddenly. Out of nowhere, everywhere, pushing aside
the arms and legs and ghosts of an ocean floor, the shades
of the dining table, Mrs. Pleasant's abrupt, unpleasant departure, "Mammy!" careened in her brain, in a *contre coup*.
Alone, she reddened, burning. She tried to quell the word.
"Mammy!" screamed once more. Then, having bested her,
it was gone.

The problem with reading, which she did profusely—"to
excess," a relation said—the problem with the thought
reading sponsored, at least to someone like her, was that
her ideas, the offspring of her mind, had no place to go.

What use was there in learning every constellation,
the configuration of every known galaxy? She had nowhere
to take her learning but into a drawing room, well ap-
pointed, comfortable or not, overwhelmed by displays of
family, the past, while the universe remained impenetrable,
black, a place of sudden upheaval.

Reading released her imagination. Pictures tumbled
forth. Disorder. Other rooms. Danger. The rabbit hole.
Come back, Alice. Chaos. Red-lined passages. Longings.
The eruption of Pele in a photograph she had once studied.
Red-hot liquid flowing out of control. Her mind. The places
it drew her to, and drew to her might astonish some.

Her cousin, Clover Hooper, now Adams, photographer of the Civil War dead, with whom she once lay side
by side on the battlefield at Antietam, while Patrick packed

the remains of the picnic and asked permission to stretch his legs, turning from the two languishing women, "There were Irish here too, you know," he said to no one—Clover had once written her, "the insane asylum seems to be the goal of every good and conscientious Bostonian."

She had to agree. Especially of the female persuasion.

What if she *had* spoken out loud the evening before? What would they have made of her? Her with her self-made mind.

Her theories arrived at in the dead of night, a pot of Earl Grey at her left hand, pale, cold.

She was loath to follow her mind out loud, not as far as it might take her. Not to herself even. Even in this room where she sat now. In her holy of holies they could still reach in, touch her, make her start.

In this room she spoke out loud only through the medium of her pet bat, Atthis, who hung upside down in the darkness under the eaves. Nourishing her nocturnal self on flies and mites and blood-weary mosquitoes.

Dearest Atthis, can you then forget all this that happened in the old days?

The book of Sapphic fragments took her back. To a country house on a hill outside Lyon, where she played chess with an old woman dressed in gray silk, sipping *vieux marc*, the residue of the old woman's own grapes, the old woman warning Alice whenever her queen was endangered: "*À la reine, ma chère!*" For the two women playing chess, the king paled beside the queen.

After the game, the old woman presented her with the

book, a silvered cover, like the old woman's silver dress. The cover fell open to a frontispiece where an artist had portrayed the Lesbian poet in *empire* style, curls piled high, breasts trapped by Napoleonic restraint.

Dearest Atthis . . . she might have been speaking to Clover, of her longing for the time they felt most alive. "Real" was the word Clover used. "For the first time, I am real."

Their longing drove them (unaccompanied but for Patrick) to Washington to review the armies of the Potomac on a summer's day under a clear blue sky, a celestial clarity that underwrote the greatness of their victory.

Roses bloomed everywhere in the nation's capital, with the fragility of old ivory, brash magenta, brilliant crimson, baby pink, pure-bred and sport alike.

Brass brands. Black contrabands. And soldiers of every regiment and stripe. The crowds lining the avenue calling out to each brigade of men, "Where from?" "Michigan!" and "Michigan!" was hollered in response. "Ohio!" "Iowa!" "Vermont!" and so on and so on. Oh, it was glorious!

The reviewing stand was decked with azaleas in full bloom. A brace of flags adorned the stand and the dignitaries upon it, each flag printed with a victorious name: Vicksburg, Shiloh, Richmond, Wilderness, Antietam, Gettysburg. The Union's finest. There they sat. Sherman, Grant, Meade. Stanton was there. And General Logan, with Indian blood streaming in his veins. One of the marching bands struck up "John Brown's Body," and some in the crowd sang along, later appending the words of Mrs. Howe.

In the midst of the procession a hatless rider with streams of golden curls swept into the crowd, apparently out of control, the scarlet scarf around his neck flapping wildly. A memorial wreath dancing around the horse's neck. Children were snatched out of harm's way. But no one felt truly endangered, such was the rider's beauty.

Someone on the sidelines whispered, "Custer."

All told, the event lasted six hours, nonstop, and when it was finished Clover and Alice retired to their quarters, the attic room of a small hotel, all that was available to a last-minute decision, as theirs had been, almost against the family will, in a city bursting at its seams.

They were exhausted, uplifted, and drifted into sleep with bedtime stories of the day, a full moon gleaming on the wallpaper surrounding them, a riot of yellow, through a skylight, admitting the city night.

That had been the Tuesday.

On the Wednesday they planned as full a day as the one before. It began auspiciously enough, with out-of-season raspberries at the breakfast table, for this was early summer. It continued with a cab ride to Ford's Theatre. But they were out of luck. There would be no viewing of Lincoln's box. In the aftermath of the president's assassination the theatre remained closed, windows and doors draped in purple and black bunting. Determined to get a sense of the place, imagine its historical moment, the two women circled the building as best they could, and found someone living in the alley out back, some sort of mixed-blood by the looks of her, tending a camp fire in the metropole, strange but articulate enough. She was poking at something in a clay pot when they came upon her.

She gave no name, but for a silver dollar (she wouldn't take paper and tested their coin against her teeth) told them the story of the night she held the reins for a man she later learned was John Wilkes Booth, having no earthly idea what he was up to.

"What sort of man did he seem?" Clover asked her.

"Ordinary." She paused. "Smaller than me."

"Besides the physical, I mean."

"Excitable."

"Did you hear anything that night?"

"Just the usual. Horses and carriages passing over the cobblestones."

"Nothing from inside the theatre?"

"Not a sound."

"Did he pay you?"

"That's as it should be."

"Wait here a moment," Clover instructed the alley dweller. "Will you?"

The woman shrugged. "I'm not going anywhere."

She returned her attention to the camp fire and the mixture which smelled strongly of game, something wild.

Patrick, their man Friday, standing by and witnessing the scene, didn't dare guess what former living thing was being stewed by this alley-dwelling woman.

He and Clover returned to the cab, which was waiting for them in front of the theatre, and he assisted in unloading her photographic equipment. Alice was left behind to make sure the alley dweller would not leave, as if she had somewhere to go.

"Would you be willing that I take your portrait?" Clover asked the woman, her back turned, her face tending a fire on a summer's day.

"Why?" the woman asked without facing the photographer.

"It's something I do."

"Your livelihood? Are you one of those shadow-catchers?" Still she did not turn around.

"No."

"Why, then?"

"I enjoy it." She was shy admitting to anyone, let alone this stranger, her artistic pretensions, as she sometimes called her drive to create. "I enjoy it," she repeated. "And you have an interesting face."

"So they tell me," came the cool response. "You are a collector of faces?"

"In a manner of speaking. May I?"

"Just like that?" She spoke the question, then paused. "I mean to say, what will you do with it? You know nothing about me; you don't know my name, and yet you want something as intimate as my likeness to take away with you. I was not born to this."

The visitors to the alley, all three, were taken aback by this individual's indignation. She had turned to face them, almost insisting they take her in, all of her. Dark chestnut hair, thick and curly, framed a well-featured face. Smudged by smoke from her fire, and ruddied by outside life, and birth, her skin was colored. Her eyes were green and remarkably clear.

Clover could not respond; she focused her eyes into the lens of her camera.

Alice spoke up:

"Please forgive us if we have offended you. My cousin and I are making a tour, in commemoration of the celebrations following the events of the past months. That's all. Our great victory. I assure you we meant no harm."

"And how do I fit into your tour, may I ask?"

"Well, you are witness to the night of President Lincoln's assassination, are you not?"

"So I said."

"As to how you came to be here," Alice went on, "we would not wish to intrude."

"Oh, intrude away! *Je vous en prie.* I'll tell you anything you want to know!"

Her eyes flashed with the dare she knew they would not accept.

"Very well," Clover said. "Patrick?"

" 'Out of the cradle endlessly rocking,' " the alley dweller quoted. "What do you think he meant by that?" she asked no one in particular. " 'Out of the cradle endlessly rocking.' "

Patrick began collecting the photographic equipment, trying to ignore the chanting alley dweller, for whom he felt embarrassment. Probably nothing a good night's sleep under a roof would not fix; the woman must be exhausted. Alone and out of doors.

" 'Twenty-eight years of womanly life, and all so lonesome.' That needs no explanation. None at all."

That stopped the visitors from departure, for the moment.

The sounds of a city morning passed into the alley but faintly, the brick buildings on either side of them serving to muffle outside noise. In their tunnel the four stood in silence, wreathed by the vapor rising from the clay pot, its sweetish smell perfuming them. Clover hoped against hope they wouldn't be offered any; she found herself concerned about hurting the woman's feelings. Alice was concentrating on the handbills posted to the brick, trying to see if an advertisement for *Our American Cousin* survived; none did.

The alley dweller broke the silence.

"I find it interesting that a man would use the number twenty-eight with regard to womanly life, and understand the lonesomeness such a life can be, don't you?"

There was an embarrassment settling on them, Clover and Alice, especially given the presence of Patrick, and a fear that this strange woman was about to begin an oration on the female cycle and Whitman's sense of it. Dear God.

"I understand that he is a good man," Alice dove in, knowing of Whitman's deeds in the war, his love of the young men he tended as nurse, as he wrote letters to their sweethearts.

"So he must be," said the alley dweller, with not at all the belligerence they had heard in her voice before. "There are some good ones, I reckon, but too few and far between. What do you think?"

How could someone such as she feel otherwise? Patrick wondered. For isn't she the picture of disappointment, of the lonesomeness of which the poet speaks? He wished the Misses Hooper would take their leave and head on to the next point of interest. Arlington, as he recalled.

The alley dweller turned to face Clover directly, staring at her until the photographer, feeling the heat of her cat's eyes, raised her head from the lens.

"I asked you a question. What do you think?"

"I beg your pardon?"

"About the human condition." She paused. "Oh, not really."

"Who are you?" Clover asked softly. Suddenly she needed to know. "How did you come to be here?"

"Do you really want to know?"

"I asked you."

"Very well. I am classified as contraband."

"I see."

"I don't think so, but that's me. A spoil of war, like the calumet Granddaddy took off a dead Creek, the cameo Grandmother got on her honeymoon in France, the jeroboam of Madeira the Yankees found in the cellar, even the kente cloth swiped by an amazon of Dahomey. All spoils. Like me."

"And how did you come to be here?"

"I was escorted by the Union army, myself among others."

"But you read."

"And. And I read."

"Yes. Poetry."

"I grant you I am an anomaly—among the contra-band, that is."

"Will you stay here?" Clover asked her.

"I will as long as I can. Unless I must run for my life."

Clover thought she knew what the woman meant, might mean, but would rather not presume.

"Are you not free?"

"Of course I am. Now we are all free. Glory, glory."

"Of course."

"But there is 'free' and then there's 'free.' "

"Your manner of speaking."

"What of it?"

"It's not what I would have expected."

"Have you never drawn close to a slave?" With that unlikely question the green eyes raked the white linen of her interlocutor.

"I was in the audience when Douglass spoke, of course. But . . ."

"Yes," the alley dweller interrupted, "an exceptional man, to be sure. What did you make of him?"

"Meaning?"

"How did he impress you?"

"He was a most effective speaker, and his cause one I believed in . . . deeply."

"Anyone else?"

"I have known free Negroes, but no, to answer your question, I have never drawn close to a slave."

"Well, you're standing next to one now."

"Where were you educated? In secret?"

"Not at my mother's breast, that I assure you. Neither at some ladies' seminary, nor in a clearing away from the patterollers."

"Seriously. Where?"

"I was taken into my father's house. He was a man of whimsy, right down to the name he gave me. I learned how to use his books, from his books I learned the significance of my name."

"And what is your name?"

"Scheherezade. The other slaves called me Sally."

"Where was your mother in all this?"

"I have not the faintest sense of her. 'Out of the cradle, endlessly searching.' Boo-hoo. She was a woman in the quarters, that's all I know. What about yours?"

"Mother?"

"That's right. You can't be the only one asking the questions, you know."

The conversation by now had eliminated Alice and Patrick. They faded into the alley, on their way back to the cab.

"No. I can't. She died when I was five years old. Of consumption."

"Who raised you?"

"For the most part my father."

"So we are both our father's daughters, and there our similarity comes to an end."

"When you speak of learning the significance of your name, what exactly do you mean?"

"You have no doubt read the *Thousand and One Nights*?"

"Indeed I have."

"Think of my father as the King of Samarkand. Instead of his wife, Scheherezade is his daughter. In my case a slave and a daughter. As long as I am his bright little monkey, I will be spared my mother's life. Allowed to roam among his books and use them. I can vacate my situation in my mind, pass through a magic casement. Wander with Marco Polo through China. With Candide through the Hundred Years' War. With Boccaccio through the Black Death. With Madame Bovary through her infidelity, witness as the arsenic burns her throat. 'She had ceased to exist.' Remember? Poor, foolish bitch. Reading. You know. Entering another's realm."

"Yes," said Clover, remembering conversations she had had with Alice and others on the selfsame subject. Being transported by words. Getting out of your skin, Alice called it. Women and books. Books and women. Boston had been appalled by the Flaubert. It was the sort of book women like her were forced to read surreptitiously, or at least in the French; sin should not be effortless. Fully grown women sneaking around, ludicrous. My God, it wasn't at all infidelity rewarded! Poor bitch indeed. Unwilling to be a woman, really, unable to be a mother and wife. A book considered poison for the young, unmarried female, as Clover was—a spinster with artistic pretensions to boot. Dangerous, like Margaret Fuller. That most unnatural being, the intellectual woman. Like her own mother, the unsigned poet, as propriety, a woman's place, demanded. The family album would be the final resting place for Clover's pictures. Strange family album, with photograph upon photograph of the dead, gravestones like babies' teeth.

"Where is he now? Your father."

"I couldn't tell you. He rode off, uniformed and sashed, his sword hanging by his side, his personal slave walking behind, carrying a basket of vittles on his head. That was the last I saw of him, about four years ago. By that time the library was no longer . . . I hesitate to call it my domain, although occasionally I imagined it into that . . . my place of being, anyway. I had been transformed into kitchen help, into Sally, taught to cook, for slave and free, guest and family. To cut meat high off the hog for the master, and low down for the slave. Encouraged to breed, but unsuccessful at that. I learned to juggle my twenty-eight days expertly. And if I was late, there were things to take. Potions brewed from leaves and berries and the like. Quite commonplace. Young girls gathered them in the wild places beyond the fields. An old woman in the quarters kept her kettle on low boil."

A spontaneous "Oh!" issued from Clover's mouth, and she felt her eyes fill. She'd only read about these things. In the narratives that filled the abolitionist libraries, in newspapers like *The North Star,* which her family took religiously. Never had she heard it told, face to face, from another woman standing an arm's length from her. Spoken with an apparent matter-of-factness that masked God-knows-what depths. She found herself trying to picture it, her with her photographic mind, but nothing real came.

"My God," she said softly, extending a gloved hand, then drawing it back in a graceful, embarrassed gesture.

"By the time he went away to the war my father had stopped speaking to me. So I don't know where he is. Can't say that I give a damn, either." If she'd noticed Clover's response, she made no sign. "And yours?"

"Mine?"

"Father."

"A physician in Boston. Eyes. As I said, he raised me and my sister. Encouraged us to participate in his life, up to a point. As girls we accompanied him on his rounds. Even to Worcester Insane Asylum, where he treated the poor unfortunates gratis, no charge to the state. They stood still for him. That's the sort of man he is."

"You can take that two ways."

Clover smiled. "Yes, I guess you can."

"Why would anyone take a child into a madhouse, I wonder?"

"My father doesn't believe in being protective."

"But did you not have nightmares?"

"Truth to tell, I don't remember."

An awkwardness settled on them like the Holy Ghost.

"I should be going. The others are waiting."

"Yes."

"We have other places to visit."

"She saw the light of day, and fell discreetly silent."

They skipped Arlington and headed for Antietam, getting there in the early evening.

On the battlefield they heard a turtle crying. Probably

the sound made by the dead, they thought, unfamiliar with the cries of turtles. They lay there after a meal of oyster loaf and white wine, while Patrick strolled the sunken road and made his way through the cornfield, imagining the green battle flags of the hell-for-leather boys of the 63rd, 69th, and 88th New York regiments, embossed with golden shamrocks and golden harps.

"Dearest Atthis," Alice spoke out loud to the small, dark figure hanging in a crevice of the room, her membranous wings tucked into her delicate body. "I do envy Mrs. Pleasant. Am I wrong to think, to say, that?"

The creature was motionless, her eyes, which might frighten some, glowed, two red spots in the dark.

"Miss Alice," a servant had warned her, "it won't do to have a bat in your room," thinking, no doubt, her mistress had one in her belfry. "For they are filthy things. Bloodsuckers and the like."

Alice had smiled in response. "Not this one, Molly. No vampire she."

The servant smiled back, one might have said indulgently, at least as indulgently as Alice had, and asserted her freedom from duties in that room.

"So be it," was her farewell.

"I envy Mrs. Pleasant her purpose, Atthis, and the movement that comes from it. 'Here I Stand, I Can Do No Other' might be engraved on her heart. That awful word engraved in my brain could not be further from the truth. I hate that it is there. She is her own woman. What an extraordinary thing to be!"

While Alice and Clover, by Alice's lights, wandered as tourists, jotting down memories, taking photographs, taking tea, looking at paintings, arranging flowers, spectating life, if that was the correct phrase. Never—but that glorious once—becoming real, descending into it, striding through it with intent.

What must that be like?

She could admit to a fantasy. My God, she allowed herself to wonder, what if we took a wagon, just the two of us, and headed west?

She'd read of female couples, the most daring of pairs, dashing in their wide-brimmed hats, friends or cousins, traveling with the wagon trains. Women homesteading in the middle of nowhere, say a prairie in Nebraska, no beginning and no end in sight, building from the ground up. Planting a cornfield. Raising a milk cow. Gathering eggs and slaughtering hogs. Shooting the eyes out of a rattlesnake.

And there the fantasy ended, with her feeling silly, having constructed but another pastime. The reality of that existence was not for the likes of her.

Unattached female, so dreadfully attached.

Imagine the Turner hanging in a sod house.

She closed the light on her writing table, picked up the letter, and in the early morning went downstairs to find Patrick and instruct him to deliver it to the Parker House posthaste.

On the High Seas, Hurricane Coming On

The rain was falling steadily as the cab approached the station, from which Mary Ellen Pleasant would take the train to New Bedford, and from there the steamer to Martha's Vineyard.

Boston steamed in the heat and wet of the August morning. The rain teemed, and the cab reflected in the waters gathering around the cobblestones. Even in the rain, the streets were crowded. The cab skidded several times as driver and horse veered around delivery boys, negotiated between businessmen, and managed to avoid others, however careless, who had a need to be downtown.

A man vending lemonade and newspaper hats on a corner was drawing a crowd, making his fortune while he demonstrated his ingenuity. Lemonade was an obvious choice to sell on a hot summer morning, but newspaper hats to keep out the rain was a stroke of genius, in a city appreciative of genius. She had the driver stop so she could buy one, always supportive of her people's enterprise, curious to see which paper the man had chosen to fold. *The Negro Voice, Serving the African-American Community Since 1827,* it declared boldly, as Bostonians caught in the downpour wore the news of postwar African-America on their heads.

"Thank you, kindly," Mary Ellen Pleasant said as she tipped the driver, hauling her frame down from the cab and gathering her carpetbag, motioning a porter to assist her with the small trunk. She held on to the newspaper hat, folding it inside the pocket of her dress.

The porter deposited her at the train with time to spare, and she settled into the overly plush first-class carriage she had reserved at the hotel.

"Thank you for your custom, madam. Please come see us again."

She opened her newspaper hat and read all about Judge Lynch and his hijinks in the countryside.

The Atlantic in the August downpour was steamy and choppy. The man at the mouth of the gangplank had warned passengers, advising them there was a hurricane on the way, and that they would be well advised to postpone their crossing if at all possible. With the Turner still burning in her mind, Mary Ellen Pleasant decided to go ahead with the crossing, as did about thirty others, mostly Methodists, heading for the campgrounds on the island to celebrate their annual revival.

Poor things, they tried to assuage the god of seasickness with a hymn-sing, and were not at all successful. Methodists in various stages of distress hung over the ship's rail, moaning and vomiting, vomiting and moaning.

Writing to Annie, heading back to her first home, the past was very much with her. Her anger last evening seemed now both justified and out of proportion, deriving not from that evening alone but from the disappointment she lived with always. The failure of their enterprise haunted her. At times a bitterness burned inside her, threatening to rise in her gullet and cut off her breath. She placed the origin of the burning in October 1859, when Harriet Tubman had been disregarded and Captain Brown seized the (wrong) day.

Harriet could see the future as clear as forever, in waking and sleeping. On the day in question, she said, her mind held "a wilderness sort of place," with rocks and scrub, where a many-headed serpent raised himself, and the eyes of each head gazed into her eyes. The blue of Captain Brown, the brown of Newby, Green, Leary, the green of Copeland. All of a sudden, from the side of the dream came a mob, with axes raised to sever the heads from the serpent. The severed heads looked at Harriet "all wishful-like," in her own words.

The message could not have been simpler, but her warning was not attended.

This is 1874, fifteen years have gone by, a war has been fought, slavery is ended: What more do you want?

Here she is, in 1874, her collaboration has gone undetected, will go to her grave with her.

She is a woman who travels first-class. She is a successful businesswoman in San Francisco, hotel keeper in that wide-open city, entrepreneur and woman of property, investor in the opening of the West: woman of the year with just the right amount of mystery to keep the sharks at bay.

She is a woman with her own mansion at 1661 Octavia Street, with a bank of eucalyptus in front she planted herself.

And her hotels were not just any hotels. And they certainly weren't whorehouses, as some of the (mostly female) gossip had it. Like that emanating from the mouth of Teresa Bell, society (such as it was) doyenne and paregoric addict, a woman who claimed to have levitated over New York City while her husband was there on business. He was rumored to be a womanizer; she said she wanted to make sure. There he was, in a banquette in Delmonico's all by his lonesome. She floated back to Russian Hill—clear across the continent—and waited to ask his forgiveness.

The devil finds work.

Lord Jesus, they take one look at a successful black woman, and they think she's either a whore or a voodoo queen. Either she got her money by sucking white cocks, or by putting spells on them.

In no way do I mean to condemn the women for whom "Westward, ho!" held a meaning other than the fulfillment of Manifest Destiny. The sisterhood is dense. From the Chinese slaves who spent their time on Gold Mountain inside a cage known as a crib; to the camp followers who landed in places named Lousetown and

Poker Flat, where they laid oilcloth at the feet of their cots, for clients too hasty to remove their boots; to the dolled-up women in the red satin and velvet bordellos of the new cities; to Dutch Hannah, fresh from combat, an original Hooker (one of the women who accompanied General Hooker's army): "Queen of the Red Light District in the Town Too Tough to Die, Laid to Rest on Boothill," so says the caption under her likeness in the "Deaths" column. "See what the boys in the backroom will have, and tell them I died of the same."

All these gals deserve a monument. To their enterprising ways. To commemorate the diaphragms they crafted from eelskin (learned from their Indian sisters?), to the douches they brewed from alum, pearlash, white oak bark, red rose leaves, nut galls, the bittertasting teas expelling the child with ease.

HERE'S TO THE WOMEN WHO SERVICED THE MEN WHO OPENED THE FRONTIER.

No, the hotels to which Mary Ellen Pleasant put her imprimatur responded to the ambitions of San Francisco to become known as the Paris of the West (as Atlanta had been, before the pyromantics of Sherman, and was becoming again, the Paris of the South; as New York City was the Paris of the North, whereas Boston remained the London, a step up from the Liverpool, in dread of becoming the Dublin; and everyone scared to death of Timbuctu).

In her establishments Mrs. Pleasant (as she preferred to be addressed, although many in the city insisted on

"Mammy") catered to those movers and shakers eager to coat their gold-dusted selves with things civilized, things brought from way around the Horn: Liebfraumilch poured into Lalique goblets, for example. Marmorean reproductions in the lobby, Harriet Hosmer's *Queen Zenobia* a favorite. Extraordinarily scented soaps in the porcelain bath. Things European.

The staff that made these enterprises (and her others) hum were strictly runagate, fugitive chattel, although by their dress and demeanor you'd never guess it. And Mrs. Pleasant took care to keep their origins secret. Should something leak, she was not above ensuring the silence of the leaker—through a well-placed bribe, warning, bullet.

One time a federal marshal, enjoying a plate of escargots (snails cultivated in the cool dark of the hotel basement) and a glass of Chambertin, was reminded of an advertisement he'd seen in the classifieds: RUNAWAY SOUGHT COFFEE-COLORED SICKLE-SHAPED SCAR ON BACK OF NECK ANSWERS TO HOSEA SURLY MANNER MISSING LOWER FRONT TEETH.

The marshal signaled the proprietress.

"Mammy, I have a need to speak to you."

"What of, Mr. Marshal?"

"That boy yonder."

"Boy?"

"The one pouring wine."

"My sommelier?"

"What?"

"The boy pouring wine."

"Yes. Where'd you get him?"

"Get him?"

"Yes, Mammy. Where'd he come from?"

"That is Louis Seize, all the way from Paris. France."

"You got a nigger all the way from France when we got so many here?"

"He's educated in wines, Marshal. Studied in the household of the Rothschilds. Surely you've heard of them?"

That stopped the marshal for the moment, but Mary Ellen Pleasant knew he knew she had tried to play him for a fool. So she secured transportation to the Pacific Northwest for Louis Seize, Hosea, where he abandoned wines and learned to ride logs down the Columbia, under the auspices of an old friend.

"I need to speak to Louis Seize [which he pronounced "seeze" in his enthusiasm]," the marshal told her on his return.

"What do you know, Marshal? I think I was deceived after all. He took off as soon as he saw you leave. I feel so foolish."

"The least you can do, Mammy . . ."

"Yes, Marshal?"

"Never mind."

Her staff was impeccably outfitted, the House of Rothschild would want no better. They served guests with a silence expected of their apparent elegance, and place, causing no stir, reminding few of the wildness of the world beyond the Golden Gate. Indian country.

Her guests were the railwaymen who blasted apart the mountains in their path, the army officers who assured their safety, the miners who scrambled over the blasted mountains, and the bankers who underwrote it all: this, the greatest enterprise the continent had ever witnessed.

She had never seen such excited men. And the landscape yielded to their excitement. The Mother Lode opened her veins for them, and bled gold into the streams.

And Mrs. Pleasant, no stranger to capital, respectful of it, moved among them naturally, as if born to the making of money. Of course, she was careful, knowing that commerce was not considered her concern. She began her empire building by embodying Mammydom, as much as she grated against the word, the notion, taking care of the guests in her hotels, washing their linen in her laundries, satisfying them in her restaurants.

To further quell any unease that she was stepping across, over, and through, Mary Ellen Pleasant dressed as a dignified, unobtrusive houseservant, no handkerchief head, but black alpaca dress, white apron, lace cap.

So she could move among them easily, in and out of any station they required. Disguised.

"How can I help you, Mammy?" a stockbroker solicitously inquired. The year was 1858.

"I'm fixin' to sell my shares in the Baltimore and Ohio; decided I don't trust money that don't look like money."

He chuckled as he was meant to, and handed over $30,000 in cash, and when she pressed him, converted it to gold, before her very eyes.

Never in a million years, not with a gun to his head, could he have guessed its destination.

Nor perceive that the woman before him, all smiles and lowered eyes, contracting into type in his mind, would be setting out the next morning for Canada, carrying a carpetbag of gold, wearing a jockey's silks. Disguised.

She wired Captain Brown ahead:

YOU WILL FIND I AM AS GOOD AS MY WORD STOP I
RIDE IN THE SECOND RACE AT CHATHAM STOP I HAVE
ALL CONFIDENCE IN OUR MOUNT STOP THE PURSE IS
YOURS STOP AS PROMISED M.E.P.

The ferryboat was heaving mightily now, and the rail was filling with trembling bodies. Methodists were praying for deliverance from the stormy blast, regretting not having stayed behind until the skies cleared. Having too much faith. The sky was pitch, almost indistinguishable from the blackness of the ocean, as the horizon disappeared.

None could get their bearings.

Mary Ellen Pleasant sipped some cognac from a silver flask, and headed further into the past.

The steamer was passing under the eye of the hurricane. Above, the sun, like an eye, stared down at them, eminently calm. But the sea was not assuaged. Black water, white-capped. The sun only clarified the fury of the water.

Looking into the water she thought of all of them, and wished her eye could pierce the blackness and see into the past below her. But she could not, and if she could, could offer them nothing.

Looking up, she had one of those thoughts she'd had as a child: that the yellow disk, impossible to stare into, as the water was impossible to stare into, that the yellow disk was the eye of God, who saw everything and forgot nothing, who was forever beyond the human gaze.

Journeyman

The first man she had loved had been her father, whose heavy-lidded eyes she had inherited. He was a seafarer, at first signing on with whalers in New Bedford and Nantucket, then becoming master of his own vessel, running along the coastline from as far away as Surinam, smuggling fresh contraband in the ship's hold. Landing at Cuttyhunk Island, Martha's Vineyard, the tip of the Cape, there offloading his cargo, barrels marked XXX, in which Africans were concealed. Which Africans then joined colonies of others runagate, scattered across the continental mass, on the islands strung along the coast, or, deciding enough is enough, some decided to piece their way back home.

The runagate settlements welcomed those willing to stay, for it was from those places that the war of the flea was being waged. Long before the costumed tragedy of the

Civil War, rebellion was a fact. These rebels concealed themselves in caves, swamps, hidden places called forts. From the Outer Banks to Sandy Ground. One such place has been recently excavated near St. Augustine. Fort Mose, which dates to the eighteenth century, was settled by slaves from the Caribbean. Earthworks, with walls topped by spikes of yucca and machete blades. The community consisted of men, women, and children who lived in thatched houses, grouped according to traditional West African "yards." Archeologists found gun flints, pieces of glass bottles, shards of pottery, animal bones. No one can tell where the people went.

There might have been one last grand stand before they melted into the Everglades, or the Big Cypress.

Captain Parsons's ship was disguised as a guineaman, a ship fitted out for the trade, and it had been used in the trade, its belowdecks shiny from human contact.

Painted on its hull and bow was a false name and a false point of origin. The H.M.S. *Daedalus,* out of Liverpool.

And how would a man of obvious darkness, you might well ask, if stopped by a patrol seeking out fugitives, explain himself as master of a ship engaged in one leg of the trade?

How could he stop them from boarding, seizing his contraband?

Never for a moment believing him.

Ah, but the trade was not monolithic.

It had happened, now and then, that a blackish boy, a Heathcliffian sort perhaps, waiting on captain and crew, was taken up, favored, taught to recognize a fish knife, the points of the compass, the use of the bit, the cat, the Book of Common Prayer, and even offered a place on the bridge. These were rare cases, mind you, and almost certainly the boy sprang from an officer, even a captain, and a favorite piece of cargo. Such a boy might grow into a master. Such a boy could buy himself into the trade.

And what would you have him do?

Offer his wrists and ankles to the blacksmith?

Her father told her his ship had been seized and searched on only three occasions. On all three, he said, the charade had been successful. The fugitives hid themselves easily in the barrels, curled into the darkness under a false bottom. No one made a sound, he told her; no one was terrified. No one was taken back to another dark, enclosed space, not the womb. Babies were dosed with paregoric (the smallest possible amount, he said) to make them sleep. No one slipped up, called out. No one panicked.

And her father, so he said, met these inspection parties with a false bill of lading, a false ship's register, a false log, a false point of origin. And with the coolness of a man who had freedom of movement all his life. And was handsome, eloquent, and furious.

Once you saw them up close, once you smelled them, you knew they were easily fooled.

So he taught his daughter.

They fell for his act, he said, hook, line, and sinker.

One inspector likened him to Othello, to which Captain Parsons responded, unveiling a huge white handkerchief, "At your service, sir!" His icicled smile lost in the inspector's delight.

The captain's success rested, no doubt, partly on his crew, who were light-skinned, green-eyed, and with one exception, inheritors of their fathers' hue. A new race for the New World. The crewmen were a few generations into it, rising into the light through categories created by Jesuits. Some reaching that place, where to the unschooled, disbelieving eye they were, for all intents and purposes, white. *Gens inconnu.* Most of the new people learned to crave lightness, but not the men of the *Daedalus.* They sought the race to which they once belonged, for which they longed.

They were a rare breed.

The one exception to the inheritors of their fathers' hue was the son of Anne Bonny, born in prison, where his mother was midwifed by Mary Reade, her partner, in crime and all else. It's a rare woman who suckles on the scaffold. Yo, ho, ho, and a bottle of rum. She moved the company and her sentence was commuted. She and Mary raised the boy in a straw-bottomed cell in Port Royal, singing him to sleep with sea chanteys, teaching him the complexity of knots, while he teethed on a piece of eight. He was taken from the two women when the governor decided, and was made a cabin boy on a Royal Navy ship. Which he jumped.

Captain Parsons found him on the waterfront.

. . .

Captain Parsons selected his crew with great care, usually through contacts in the skein of islands stretching from Trinidad to Cuba. The pirate child was an exception. The captain named him Jimmy and took him as his own.

When Captain Parsons offered the boarding parties a dram of the finest Jamaican slave-made rum, they lapped it up.

"Gentlemen, I give you the trade, and our success in it!"

His voice boomed into the hold, momentarily rattling a few.

In gratitude and with equal enthusiasm, the leader of the boarding party raised his glass to the toast, clinking with the captain of African descent, looking into his heavy-lidded eyes, captivated by him, not noticing as a knife, freshly honed and shined, entered the place under his heart and drew the life out of him. The crew followed suit with the rest of the boarding party and soon it was over. The bodies going down, down, down, to join the others. The contraband relaxed as the all-clear sounded.

Such were the stories the captain gave his daughter. Never fear, never panic, never "hey-nigger-stand-and-deliver."

No runagate smothering from the heaviness of the sugar smell in the hold. The nipple on which the paregoric was dribbled always belonged to the baby's mother; at least, he never told her otherwise.

He needed to pass his version on.

He needed to protect her from the world.

Years later, when the *San Francisco Elevator* interviewed her about her legend of a father, she repeated his stories by heart, knowing all along there was much more to it—how could there not be?—but knowing, she thought, what was good for the people.

In the barracoons of the Caribbean his free-born origins went for nought. Each body stepping down the gangplank, each neck in each coffle, each figure in the bloodless cutaway of the slave ship's hold (said by one fanciful trader to resemble "books on a shelf") had been free-born.

It did not matter that he was used to freedom.

He could be seized as easily as that.

One night he was.

He'd landed the *Daedalus* in Montego Bay. One of those places where the trade reached its apotheosis, overlooking a perfect sea, where moonlight lit the canefields, and shone across the auctioneer's platform, so bright you could read accounts by it, highlighting ebony skin, while the tradewinds gently assisted guineamen into a superb, if crowded, harbor. What a place! What commerce!

Breathtaking in its situation. Morning, noon, and night there was movement on the docks.

"Evening, Captain Parsons," the pilot greeted him.

"Good evening, Mr. Evans."

"Here for a new shipment, are you?"

"Yes, indeed."

"Must like their rum in New England, then?"

"It's a cold, cold place, Mr. Evans. Warms the cockles."

Attention paid, he tipped Mr. Evans and went on his way.

The Cage, as it was known, was downtown, not far from Palmer's Wharf.

The Cage still stands today, having endured for several centuries in several guises. First as a holding pen, then as a clinic, dispensary, the office of the Montego Bay Chamber of Commerce, a travel agency, and, finally, a museum. As God is my witness.

In the beginning the Cage had been wood, but its inhabitants, in their desire to free themselves, damaged it severely, pushing the walls outward, collapsing the structure. The remains of this first Cage were demolished and replaced by one of limestone, mortared, as so many buildings were, with King Sugar. Solid as a rock, and almost soundproof to the outside world, which was important, since the Africans often set to calling themselves home, howling through the day and night.

A red hibiscus rose along one side of the building, and a brilliant bougainvillea climbed the wall along the other.

Inside, the place was stark, dirt for a floor, a tub of shiny ordure stood in the center of the room. / / / / / / / /—the counting out of time perhaps—were slashed in the mortar between the stones.

In other places, more delicate engravings survived:

o ∘+∘ o

Richard Parsons landed in the Cage after meeting with a sympathetic Carib in the back room of a tavern by the docks.

The Red Coats killed the Carib, who was supposed to be extinct anyway.

And they apprehended Captain Parsons for being in the wrong place at the wrong time. They tore his free papers in half, declaring them forgeries. They seized his purse, regarding the contents as thievery. Whatever they said, went. "Who steals my purse, steals trash" earned him a slap that made his teeth sing.

And so he became a runaway slave.

"What do they call you, nigger?"

Captain Parsons, runner of contraband people, told the soldiers his name was Arthur Wellington. His ally was dead; his head was ringing. He was beyond cautiousness.

The lieutenant commanding the party was not amused.

"I've heard of Africans called Hercules and Plato and Hamlet, but never one calling the name of the Iron Duke in vain. Your massah would not dare. What's your real name, eh? And don't give me any mumbo-jumbo."

He pictured the Carib blood running into the rum on the tavern floor. Just like that. Just like that a man with pictures on his skin had his heart explode. Captain Parsons could not weep for him in front of these men.

"I'm known as Wilberforce, Lieutenant."

"Like hell you are."

"What's in a name, Lieutenant? A rose by any other name would smell as sweet. They call me 'Romeo.' "

"That's more like it. Come along, Romeo."

This Red Coat had a fascination with his own voice. He carried on almost nonstop on the march to the Cage, remarking on the softness of the tropical night, the scent of night-blooming jasmine, what he called the "hot constitutions" of Africans, by which he did not mean the state papers of Dahomey or Angola.

"Maybe that's why they call you Romeo, eh, Romeo?"

The lieutenant described his journeys to the Slave Coast and how few of his mates had survived the Bight of Benin. He told "Romeo" he should be grateful: "Lucky we found you when we did, Romeo, else that Carib might have had you for supper."

Ye gods!

Ever since the Admiral of the Ocean Sea had christened the people *caníbal,* and Shakespeare anagrammatized them to Caliban, their fate was dealt.

Soon all that would be left of them would be the name of the perfect sea, and pickled cicatrices in a natural history museum.

Captain Parsons longed to tell the lieutenant about the Capuchin found in a town square simmering half a child along with some callaloo. He did not dare.

The lieutenant had forsaken the Carib and moved on to what or whom "Romeo" might be expected to encounter in the Cage.

"I hear there are several women in there. But before you try to live up to your name, beware. These are women who attempted to *dunbar* their overseer. You know what that means, don't you, Romeo?"

"Romeo" looked blank.

"It means murder. A style of killing particularly suited to females. In the night, silently. Without a chance for the victim to prepare to meet his god. The name of some poor devil whose slaves—women all—murdered him in his own bed." The lieutenant stressed the last two words, as if that made it all the more beastly.

"Slaves—women all—" echoed through "Romeo." He recalled the words of a slaver he'd overheard that evening in the tavern. The slaver was describing a recent voyage to the mouth of the Niger; his ship had become damaged. While the repairs were being done, the man had time on his hands. "Purchased a girl for myself," he said.

You could never get used to such words.

"These African females are illustrious viragoes, Lieutenant," the sergeant said, with the savor of a man who loved to coin a phrase and thought he was good at it.

"They are indeed, Sergeant."

"Their leader is a slave named Mesopotamia. They say she has a hole in her ear where the overseer nailed her to a tree."

"What offense, Sergeant?"

Did she claim to be the Son of God? "Romeo" wondered.

"The usual, Lieutenant. Refusal to breed."

"Like hens who refuse to lay when not satisfied with their situation, Sergeant."

The sergeant chuckled.

"They caught her passing out doses of wild cassava to the others as well, Lieutenant." The sergeant named a favorite abortifacient.

"So they nailed her to a mahogany and she hatched the plot from there." The sergeant was tickled with his wordplay.

"Well, then." The lieutenant paused. "Incorrigible."

"Romeo" had said nothing.

In the tavern they had been talking about what drove them, how they kept on despite all they had witnessed, all they looked forward to. To each other they admitted despair, to furious brainstorms, dulled only barely by rum.

What kept them going?

People. Their own. That's all they had.

The pictures on the red-gold skin moved as the Carib gestured. Their black eyes met, and they touched hands.

And into this intimacy the Red Coats strolled, casually storming the room, interrupting two men falling into love, and before Captain Parsons could say goodbye, the moving pictures were still, and he was clapped in irons.

They tossed him into the darkness of the Cage, where an unbearable stench enveloped him. Where he sought company. A woman with a hole in her ear, named for the cradle of civilization, whose Babylon had been known for its hanging gardens.

Allusions to civilization were everywhere.

The miasma was making him light-headed, and he

tried to picture her garlanded with hibiscus and the blossoms of the wild cassava she dispensed, bringing those scents into competition with the stench of the Cage.

Slave names could be a guide to the enthusiasms of masters. When her master beheld Mesopotamia, called for her, of what was he reminded?

A schoolmaster's lessons about the ancient world?

A glorious dark-skinned empire, now enchained?

The Church of England? Being flogged by a master for a wet dream?

The Revelation to John?

Fagging? Kneeling on flagstones, freezing?

"The Mother of harlots and earth's abominations?"

Captain Parsons sought her company in the Cage, but Mesopotamia and her sisters were long gone. Even now decorating the canefields, feeding the vultures known as John Crow, shiny black and hungry.

Some people believed that slaves punished to death came back as John Crow. This could not have been true, for the skies of the island would have been black, not blue.

But some people persisted, explaining the Crow-them eat the slave-them, and then the slave-them become the Crow-them and fly all the way back to Africa; is true-true.

And then what? Nyam dead hyena for time everlasting?

Nuh, man, nuh tu'n back into warrior-them?

And then the sweet sound of air hitting teeth.

Disbelief. But the longing for a return, to Africa, life, home.

Captain Parsons sat against the wall and ran his forefinger over the slashes in the mortar. He recognized / / / / / / / as someone's attempt to calculate time, but the ∘ ⊹ ∘ was beyond his understanding.

Born African in the New World he was too many generations removed from the four moments of the sun. Someone—Mesopotamia?—was not.

Captain Parsons survived because survival is random and he was lucky. Jimmy managed to trace him to the Cage, and claimed him as lost property.

Turtle Crawle

Cinnamon women dug pens where the river entered the sea. In these they domesticated great green turtles. White beach on either side of the crawle, where the turtles buried their eggs.

The cayman slid around the crawle wondering why he too was not penned.

He was not for egg-bearing. He caught an arrow in the back of his throat, and the women dried his flesh over a fire and dried his skin in the sun.

The women picked oysters off the stems of mangroves and slid a tempered, sharpened knife of stone between the lips of the shell, slicing the muscle, the shell laid open.

The midden grew.

Mother-of-pearl glistened in the pile.

They made soup in calabashes with dasheen and callaloo, thickened with cassava, flavored with coconut milk.

They called the cassava *yuca* and believed, more than in any other living thing, the power of their Supreme Being was captured in it.

They called the silk cotton tree, from which they carved their canoes, the Tree of God.

The tree grew tall enough to guide the boats home, and the wood was light enough to hold a hundred people on the high seas. In these canoes the people traveled everywhere, met each other, along the African coast, through the chains of the South Pacific, verging the ice cliffs of Antarctica. In these canoes the people read the stars, made great sweeps across currents; wherever there were stars and water, they went.

The cinnamon women spoke only Arawak, a custom which began as an act of defiance. Many Carib women became Carib as a result of raids on Arawak settlements.

They held to their tongue.

The women were stonecutters, lapidaries. They carved the *zemi*, the individual god possessed by each member of the tribe.

Imagine having your own god.

Cinnamon men carved flutes from the bones of their enemies.

They were the musicians. They were the navigators.

The men had a secret dialect with which to plan war.

Cinnamon men cried into battle at midnight, blowing their war conches, smeared with white powder made from the claws of wildcats, swinging their war clubs over their heads in wide arcs.

The island sang with their noise.

Can you imagine all these sounds?

Cinnamon men smeared white crying into battle in the middle of a tropical night.

Flute songs.

The carving of stone.

Turtle song.

Language.

Can you imagine?

The landscape before the [land]fall [of Colón]?

The people.

The rush of water against the side of a canoe.

The clarity of the night sky.

The salt caked in the carvings.

The astronomer reading the night.

Some petroglyphs are left as evidence.

From when the world was soft and the people could leave hand and foot prints on rock. From cinnamon women who carved human figures with plumes haloing their heads, turtles swimming, a cayman with a fish in his mouth, evoking a private god.

Words.

potAto

hurRicane

tobAcco

W

bArbecue

hammocK
a
n
o
e

Among the people the stages of life were incised on the skin. The hieroglyphics formed symbols understood only to initiates. As with the Kongo cosmogram encountered by Captain Parsons in the mortar of the Cage.

Before Captain Parsons took his leave of Jamaica, he sailed to the south coast to find the Carib settlement at Milk River, one of three turtle crawles where there had once been hundreds. There he would inform the people of the death of another of their number. At least that was his intent.

Cultivation was edging them. Through a screen of green not a hundred yards behind them a stone-fenced field was visible, with several chestnut horses grazing against a sky Constable might have painted.

The people stood at the verge of the sea. Captain Parsons approached them through the waves, rowing in alone in his ship's tender.

A line of men, and one woman, met him at the water's edge.

They seemed exhausted. And sat down then and there, passing a calabash of rum between them.

The woman spoke, holding out the calabash to him. "You are Parsons."

There was no question in her tone.

"Yes."

"We know you."

"I am the bearer of very sad news," he said, realizing the declaration was unnecessary.

As they drank, the giant turtles, great female beasts, so old they might remember pre-contact days, might miss the prior landscape, might know what had been, where the canefields, and indigo plants, and coffee pieces, and herds of Brahman cattle now were. They might remember what had been transplanted when Captain Bligh put in his bread-fruit trees.

The turtles swam to and fro through the river water mixed with sea, back and forth, as a cayman slid past the crawle.

Quasheba

The first woman Mary Ellen Pleasant had loved had been her mother, Quasheba.

Quasheba taught her daughter the need for movement, even as a woman, especially as a woman. Movement in the sense of moving against, against, and toward, and away, and across, but not in circles, that was the danger, to go around and around and around.

When Quasheba was little and afraid of storms, and convinced the ocean would wash over the dunes of the Sea Islands and wash her away, her own mother taught her about Yemaya, who was mother of the seas, and whose responsibility the churning waters were.

"But why is she so angry, Ma?"

"Too many of her children are at the bottom of the water."

"Why doesn't she stop it?"

"She can't."

"If she rules the sea?"

"It is beyond her."

On a clear day from the highest dune you could see the Guinea Coast, and all the traffic in between. The skin of the globe tightened and over the curve ships came, rushed, lying low in the water, eager to make landfall. Quasheba's mother described the procession to her daughter, the colors streaming from the masts that held the sails. Try as she could, the little girl could not make them out.

"Use your imagination," her mother said. "Every single day a shipload leaves from the coast. At least."

Once, trying hard to see what her mother promised, Quasheba thought she glimpsed the top of a mast, way way out, a man in a straw hat on watch. Why the hat didn't blow into the sea she could not say, unless her vision was a child's fancy.

"This is as far as we go; I don't care," her mother said. "This is bad enough, but at least we can keep track of home. We stay here," she declared, knowing she had no say about her coming and going. She stood on the dune keeping watch, a whooping crane with her back to the mainland.

When lightning lit the sky and thunder bombarded her in her bed, her mother told her about Shàngó, who carried lightning bolts in her fists, his fists, and meteorites on his head, her head, who rumbled through the heavens morning, noon, and night.

"Why doesn't he do something, Ma?" Quasheba asked.

Why don't her lightning bolts split the facade of the

great house? Why doesn't he set fire to the bales stacked on the docks in Charleston? Why was the end of her fury always burning bushes, haystacks, the thatched roofs of the quarters? Why doesn't he fire a meteorite into the ballroom one fine summer night and scare them all to death?

"He can't; she can't."

There it was: the admission that the transoceanic, African, eclipse-demanding, vengeance-hungry gods were helpless.

In the end they became beautiful stories, dazzling imagery, the stuff of bedtime excitement and children's language, figures drawn with a pointed stick in the sand— useless. A female riding the foam, swinging low on a chariot of *abeng*, in a blue garment flowing into the waves, alive with stars, could not hold her own. Against the endless canvas of sails, the passing of cargo, the genius for detail, this pretty picture was powerless.

Who could have imagined the extent of it? Not even those who had the power to imagine the breath-taking gods.

What to do with these depressed gods? Who will end up in a botanica behind gated windows, next to a storefront church where Jesus drops the charges. Salted codfish soaks in a basin in the back room. On the counter, a candle lit to Shàngó inspires a lottery ticket. The smell of sea and melting wax and the artificial scent which clings to Shàngó overwhelms the other gods. The Virgin of Guadelupe, Indigenous Mother of the Americas, wrinkles her nose; Shàngó smells like an overripe peach.

On a street beyond the gated windows a crack-skinny woman yells "Bitch!" to no one in particular. She is transfixed, her eyes look to the heavens for a trick, a fix. She will wait, leaning against a tombstone in the old cemetery on Zion Street, graven in letters spelling In Memoriam.

As soon as she was old enough by her mother's lights, Quasheba was sent away from the islands, north to another.

She left on the *Daedalus,* headed for Martha's Vineyard to learn her craft, which occasioned her meeting Captain Parsons, with whom she later had their daughter.

Her departure was forced by the advances of the master, and she left her beloved islands and her beloved mother and her beloved Gullah tongue behind.

It was on Martha's Vineyard that Quasheba became the pupil of Ogún, master smith. She was taught by him to forge gunmetal; she learned to make a decent firearm.

Quasheba was again on Martha's Vineyard when her daughter was born. In a few weeks she was off again. The baby slung in a kente cloth across her chest, leather satchel with the tools of her trade in her left hand, carpetbag with a change of clothes and baby linen in her right.

She was walking to a Maroon settlement in the Berkshire Hills, nearby Tanglewood. Spring was on the verge, the moment when green exploded nearing, and she was pointing out its signs to her newborn daughter. Leaning against the silvered trunk of a birch at the side of the road, a nest of evening grosbeaks twitting overhead. She bent down and picked a ladyslipper, tickling the baby under her nose with the bloom. The baby stirred, then settled farther into the cloth sling, and sleep.

Quasheba talked to her daughter the entire trip. Walking into Stockbridge, she taught Mary Ellen (whom Richard Parsons wanted to name Mesopotamia, but wouldn't tell why; Quasheba chose for her daughter an unobtrusive name, for public use, and an obtrusive, secret one, which went with Mary Ellen Pleasant to her grave. No one was still alive who called her by it, whispered it next to her sleeping head.), she taught her baby about Mum Bett, dropping the browning ladyslipper on the old woman's grave, next to the Sedgwick family dog.

The Maroon settlement was concealed in a forest above the Housatonic, overlooking the Appalachian Trail. There the people held a nine-night ceremony for the baby, in which her obtrusive, secret name was spoken, in which she received her soul. In turn Quasheba thanked them, then spoke to them of the alchemical source of gunpowder, reciting the treatise of the Ethiopian magus, Trismegistus, by heart, as Ogún had taught her, lit by the moonlight of the New England night. She taught them the exact proportions necessary to explode saltpeter, sulfur, carbon. Telling them that if you increased the amount of saltpeter you increased the speed of combustion, the quickness of explosion, extending the flash of light.

While she spoke, the people passed her newborn daughter hand to hand.

And so they went, that first year of Mary Ellen's life, and the second, and the third.

By the fourth, Mary Ellen was enrolled in a Free African School on Martha's Vineyard. When Quasheba was killed in a raid on the Great Dismal Swamp in 1825, her daughter was fourteen. Mary Ellen was given her mother's hand-wrought revolver, which, in all her days, never left her side.

"The axe is laid at the foot of the tree."

August 6, 1874

Dearest Annie,

Here I sit, in the saloon of a steamer bound for the Vineyard, taking pen in hand to speak with you again. Strange, since before yesterday's letter to you, I'd not been much of a correspondent. But on this journey you have become my companion, as once you were long ago. Comrade-in-arms. I need a seasoned ear as I journey back. Why does travel make one reflect on the past so?

It does me. I could have the most fascinating book in front of me and inevitably my mind marches back. The sight of wagon ruts from my train window on the journey east set off a chain of memories. A woman I knew once, laundress in one of my hotels, who told me of her terror on the trail. Not of Indians, or rattlesnakes, just the terror of wide-open spaces. "I don't trust a place I can't measure," she said. So frightened was she that she set fire to the wagon, losing all her belongings, and her husband (he'd had enough of her, she said) in the conflagration. Saw everything go up. Including the lilac she'd uprooted from their New England dooryard, packed with dirt and burlap.

After that she walked, hitching a ride now and then, in exchange for help with chores. "When I walked it," she told me, "I fit more into the country than when I rode over it. It may sound crazy, but that's how I felt. And I could stop and wonder at all of it. No need to hurry up. From the wagon there was mostly scrub as far as the eye could see. On the ground was another matter. Tiny, shy flowers, the elegance of scorpions, spiders, dewdrops, birdcalls. I grew to love it."

The ruts from the train window brought her back, her words intact.

"A place I can't measure." I guess that's the way I feel about the ocean, across and especially beneath.

And the past.

I hope this letter writing is not too much of an imposition on you. I mean that sincerely, without a trace of the sarcasm on which (part of) my reputation rests.

Who knows? I may not even post this.

But you are to me like an old lover; don't be shocked. I mean you know me very well and can read between the lines. There is no one left who can.

Let me draw the scene for you.

On the ship, lacing the deck, are violently ill people,

on their way to a religious revival. We have passed through a fierce storm, and the sea is choppy at best. Their god apparently has forsaken them. I soon enough retreated inside, knowing the saloon would be nicely deserted and I could have it to myself—which of course pleases me.

I sit in a comfortable armchair, black leather, before a mahogany writing desk, lit by a green-shaded lamp. Not to worry, the lamp is fixed to the desk securely, by finely polished brass fittings.

As the ship pitches and rolls, the lamp does not budge. I can smell the whale oil which causes the light, the beast rendered for human needs.

I am drawn back to my father's stories of his whaling days, before he joined the Cause. I remember him telling me how the ship stank to its heart as the beast was melted down.

I, of course, as a little girl was only interested in whether they found anyone—any person, that is—living inside. I had a childish picture of a whale's belly as cavelike, with ribs like exposed beams. It would be dark unless light escaped down the waterspout, unless there was an oil lamp, on a table, next to a captain's chair.

My father smiled at my imaginings, and told me that a whale's belly drew light from clouds of phosphorescent plankton. "Like swallowing a thousand fireflies," he said.

I have no idea if this is scientific fact, but it made a beautiful picture.

"Like having shooting stars inside of you," Quasheba added.

I remember the scene vividly—one of the few times we three were together.

When I asked, "Captain Parsons, did you find Jonah?"

He responded, "No, my dear, not in a whale, but in the belly of another beast."

I was too young to catch his reference to the Trade, and pressed for the story of another beast. He went along, saying that once they'd caught a great white off Nantucket with a seaman's papers stuck in his gullet.

No other trace of the sailor.

No one could say what happened, but certainly the poor man had drowned, he said.

"Or been eaten?" I asked with a child's excitement at such goings-on.

"Or been eaten."

And with that, and the vomiting Methodists as Greek chorus, I am taken suddenly back to last evening, of which I wrote you, and the disembodied leg and fish in the Turner painting.

A past immeasurable, indeed.

I encountered someone in the Parker House dining room this morning, from another place. I cannot get him out of my mind; it feels like I never will. We spoke, yet didn't speak. No, he was not a foreigner. And I'd better go no further, for if I do mail this, you may think me mad. Then again, my dear, your people are rife with *obeah*, spirit, second sight, so you might actually understand. I'm not sure I do.

The crew has taken note of the fact that I seem not

in the least disturbed by the storm, and that I demonstrate the sea legs of one used to voyages. Not knowing my history, and assuming what comes to them readily with regard to women of my obvious descent, I can almost hear them whisper "voodoo."

Why am I not afraid?

For aren't our people to be terrified of water? The wrath of God?

What nonsense! Though God knows we have reason.

Still, at times like these "voodoo" can be a blessing. For they cut me a wide swath and the service is good. (Smile.)

"The axe is laid at the foot of the tree."

Remember?

I am drawn back into my own peculiar past. I look out over the blackness of the water, and find myself not on the high seas, heading for the Vineyard in 1874, but see a girl, as clear as day, a young woman, participant at Chatham, captivating. You. Listening to Mary Shadd Carey urge us on in the colored (coloured?) schoolhouse where so much of the planning took place. You in your mannish overalls, your face darkened, but you could not hide your eyes.

Where are you now, Annie?

The last time you wrote me, it seems like years ago and probably was, you spoke of your lepers, visiting them, the closest thing to the nunnery your mother urged you toward. Are you still there?

You are a young woman. Don't bury yourself there.

Where are you in your heart?

Is it broken? Still?

I don't like to think of you there with a broken heart.

You are the closest thing I ever had to a daughter.

We came so damn close. I know your disappointment—weak word—was tremendous, but, well, you know . . .

The cognac is excellent. But Napoleon brandy, not Toussaint brandy. (Smile.)

I get very fed up.

I get very fed up with everyone referring to our enterprise as "John Brown's Raid on Harper's Ferry." I get very fed up with the engravings in history books. J. B. as a stark raving mad Moses; to do what he did, you'd have to be "tetched," I guess.

I do not crave notoriety, God knows. If they'd been able to put two and two together I'd have swung alongside the captain and the others. I do not want fame, truly, or ownership of history, for that matter, but the official version is a cheat.

But then, what's to be done? The winner names the age. Renaissance, Enlightenment, Age of Reason.

But then again, even when we are the winners—not of ages, my dear, of certain moments—our victories are not recorded, not really.

Spirituals, not war chants; laments, not battle cries.

Liberation is not achieved; it is handed down.

What if last night Miss Hooper and the gathered company could read my memory, all of it? And find I am not tame? That I have committed acts that would shock them, to put it mildly.

That's how we're seen. Long-suffering. And more. Sweet Jesus, why am I telling you this?

My mother's gun is tucked into my skirt.

How few are left who ever heard her name. Or knew what she was about.

This is delicious: What if last night I'd emptied my mother's chambers into Mr. Turner's painting? Can you imagine it?

The official version is for public consumption—in both senses of that word.

Why should I care, or be surprised? I'm well set, considered powerful by enough people. I matter. And I have never been tamed. I may pay for that someday.

Merde, à la trente fort.

I do care. World-weary, hardtack-toughened as I am. And with the knowledge that were the real story known, and believed, my enterprises in San Francisco, which drive our efforts in the Golden State, would be at serious risk.

At first they'd find it hard to swallow, to be sure.

I can hear the city fathers now: "Our Mammy? Armed and dangerous? Not our Mammy."

Then I say to myself, give it up: Success was not ours in any case. Not the way I measure it.

And yes, my dear, I will go into the ground wondering, What happened? Why was I greeted on the road to Charleston, fifty-two rifles concealed in the back of the wagon, dressed as an itinerant blacksmith, by a messenger telling me Harper's Ferry was a fiasco, everyone was dead, and if I knew what was best for me I would make tracks myself. At first I didn't trust the man, but then he spoke to me in code so I had no choice but to believe him. I left the rifles in his care, thanked him, and began to walk north.

I don't think I had ever been more frightened than on that journey. I had been born into freedom. I had been protected by my mother and my father. I had been loved by my dear husband, James. And here I was, just like that, my mother's gun the only thing between me and it.

And the signs of it were everywhere, of course.

I was terrified of eye contact. That whites would read my fury. So I walked with my head down, acting dumb.

I began dragging my left leg, feigning a poor prospect for a slave.

Neither could I look black people in the eye. With our failure I felt a huge remorse; I couldn't face those I failed.

I worried about you. *Everyone was dead* reverberated in my mind. Which *everyone*? The everyone at the armory, in the countryside, on the roads? Was the messenger well informed? Or had the news spread south gathering casualties?

Where were you? I couldn't even remember where you were supposed to be.

Where did the signals get crossed? Why did J. B. jump the gun? What told him to?

Dear God, a poster in the corner of the saloon has caught my eye. JACK SAMPSON, ETHIOPIAN DELINEATOR EXTRAORDINAIRE, then, in less bold type, APPEARING NIGHTLY.

Why did J. B. not heed dear Harriet's words?

Some white boys tried to take me. It must have been about Virginia. I was trying to find my way to Portsmouth, to Eliza Bains, the slave woman who sent slaves north by boat. She'd got my father involved all that time ago, and as far as I knew was still alive, active. I was in the middle of some woods, when three boys appeared in front of me, blocking my way.

Apparently they wanted some amusement.

They wanted this "one-legged nigger" as they called me to dance for them. Just a little "Jump, Jim Crow."

They couldn't have been more than twelve or thirteen, but they had learned their lessons well. One of them was trailing a length of rope behind him. I had no choice.

Well, honey, they didn't know what hit them.

I dumped the sons of the South in a ditch, securing them to each other with rope around their necks. I covered them with some brush and set them ablaze. Before I made tracks I tacked a note to a tree nearby:

THESE WERE SOME MEAN NIGGERS. YOU OWE ME A FAVOR.

SIGNED,

A GENTLEMAN.

I walked farther north, the smoke from their burning bodies at my back.

I never did find Eliza Bains.

I turned myself back into a woman in New York City, where I caught a ship back home.

You should be here *now*.

A huge wave has just washed over us. Not quite a tsunami, but close enough. Truly. Someone had better do a Methodist head count.

But where is our Ethiopian Delineator Extraordinaire? Has his blackface washed away?

I do hope I catch a glimpse of him.

Our witnesses will soon enough be gone.

Yes, my dear, we might as well give it up, our telling of the past.

We own but a few of the presses. We wield no power in the mills that train the minds, unless you count the power to stoke the furnace, turn down the beds, make sure the chicken isn't bloody.

The failed revolutionary is claimed by them as one of them. A prodigal son. Profligate dreamer who instigated an American nightmare. What else are they to do with Captain Brown? Their wild-haired, wild-eyed boy determined to save the darkies, at the expense of family and fortune, and general social standing.

What a farce!

J. B. was a splendid ally; no more, no less.

But why do I preach to you about this, Annie? You were there, your eyes on fire. You know full well.

Fire, indeed, said the hologrammatical man in wonder at the ditch, the burning.

Not you, not now. You're disturbing my train of thought, M.E.P. said in silence.

Forgive me. I am slightly awed by you, what you're saying.

Please, let me get this letter over with. The sea is beginning to get to me, even to me.

Why didn't I know you? About you?

My point exactly.

That Canadian spring. Lilacs late. Meetings, conventions, a constitution for a state within a state. I know you know all this, but sometimes I feel the need to say it out loud, write it down, before I begin to disbelieve it, before my own amnesia sets in.

I probably should have had children. Since I didn't, you will have to do; be my heir. I say this knowing *heiress* is not your favored calling. I bequeath to you the story of my life.

J. B. and I had our differences, true. We clashed horribly at Chatham, but we managed to keep our argument private.

The cause of our disagreement?

Ye gods. In the midst of this, my writing to you, dredging my mind, a not-dead, not-alive man by my side (the less said about that, the better), the ocean and heaven in apparent uprising, the Ethiopian Delineator is setting up shop in his corner of the saloon, putting a smashed-down top hat on his head, and spreading sand on the stage, moving his feet in a studied lackadaisicality, against the motion of the ship. Jump, Jim Crow.

No, Captain Brown and I almost fell out—and had our enterprise succeeded it would have been interesting to see what would have happened, who would have prevailed—we almost fell out over his devotion to communism, his notion of an African state as a christo-utopia, a heaven on earth for colored folks.

That did not wash with me.

We'd been discussing what should be done once our victory was complete; we were caught in a revolutionary dreamtime.

I objected to his notion immediately. Dammit, our people knew capitalism intimately, historically. Albeit from the wrong end—at least in the New World. I reminded him that in Africa commerce came easily to us, there were no communist states, no states of noble savagery. We clashed like cymbals, he and I. And I accused him of pedestalizing the African, a practice as potentially degrading, and damaging, as enslavement.

Monsieur Sampson is elaborately mouthing—and, Lord Jesus, I do mean mouthing—something or other on the stage, which pitches and tosses. A buck-and-a-wing in a gale.

What was wrong, I asked Captain Brown, with slaves seizing that which they built, dug, cultivated, designed, maintained, invented, birthed, for which they had been held responsible?

Hadn't they achieved ownership in kind?

I worried, as I told him, that he saw our people's experience as somehow ennobling; that we were *better* than capitalism, since we had been crucified by it. Were we now to roll back the stone and ascend from a netherworld into utopia?

"But, my dear friend," he responded to my concern, "why is private property so important to you?"

"Because in this world, Captain, property, ownership equals power. And in this world, I cannot and do not wish to contemplate the next, we need as much power as we can get. We are not an otherworldly people, Captain. We are of this world and this time."

"But does the Trade not prove the end result of capitalist endeavor?"

"The Trade was an extreme made reasonable. We need not behave in like manner. We do not wish to enslave the enslavers, Captain. Only to take what we have earned and apply it to our future."

"You are talking about the redistribution of wealth."

"Why shouldn't I?"

"Mrs. Pleasant, you are the most practical human being I have ever known, male or female."

I nodded, as ladylike as possible.

"Surely," he went on, "you realize such an enterprise is doomed to fail. Any white allies we may acquire will fall away. Liberation is one thing. Seizure of private property something else entirely."

"My God, Captain, if nothing else, my practicality teaches that the limits of that particular alliance can stop well short of our overstepping any artificial economic bounds."

"Yes. I know."

"We cannot be in the business of seeking approval. Waiting on others to join us, to come along and be saved.

What is the difference, may I ask, between arming the slaves with firearms, causing insurrection, as we have planned, and seizing and redistributing property? Both involve violent means; both are entirely justified."

"One is immediate, and may be understood as a logical outcome of enforced servitude, a sensible, a *human* response to it—by some at least."

"By few, Captain. Of that ilk at least."

"I don't know."

"Think about it. When the white man responds to oppression, it is expected that he will struggle against it, use any means necessary to liberate himself. For the African, the expectation has never been the same. To hear a black man utter the words, 'by any means necessary,' would do nothing but strike terror in the white heart. It is not expected of us."

She lifted her head, and hand, from the paper, and the past, and saw the glint of spectacles, and the trace of a smile across the room, where the hologrammatical man leaned against a billiard table, tossing the cue ball between his left hand and his right.

Captain Brown continued to resist Mrs. Pleasant's notion of ownership, of seizing private property.

"That would threaten the entire landscape, and would send this country into chaos, and bring down protracted war upon us."

No more chaotic than this room, this ship, at this moment.

I do believe it's my turn to break, the hologrammatical man said, addressing the Delineator. He made no sign he heard, shuffling his feet, hunching his shoulders forward, singing, if you could call it that, but unable to hear his own voice, to breach the noise of the ocean. Jump down, spin around, pick a bale of cotton / Jump down, spin around, pick a bale of hay / Me and my gal gonna pick a bale of cotton / Me and my gal gonna pick a bale of hay.

There was a crack! in the song, as the balls broke apart from the triangle and scattered across the green. It appeared the hologrammatical man would play the solids.

"Perhaps we need to take that chance; perhaps a protracted war of liberation is the only way."

"We are outnumbered."

"But freedom without the means to be self-supporting is a one-armed triumph. Hopeless, and will earn us no respect."

"Do you speak of respect or retribution?"

R-E-S-P-E-C-T sang the hologrammatical man as he chalked his cuestick.

For pity's sake, she pleaded with her company.

I'm sorry, he said, leaning back against the table, his arms folded across his chest. Forgive me, I'm a very young man.

Now, where was I?

Respect or retribution?

Oh, yes.

"You know, Captain, without my particular expertise at ownership, property, there would be no thirty thousand dollars in gold, no rifles for our people. And that money was made in disguise, in the dark, so to speak. I would like to step into the open, for once. All of us."

"For your expertise with profit, your generosity, we are all grateful, Mrs. Pleasant."

"Generosity has absolutely nothing to do with it, Captain. What else would I do?"

"And what of afterward?"

"Afterward?"

"After the gunfire has dissipated, the plantations seized, the factories occupied, the banks burned to the ground."

"And the babies seized from the breast and paraded on pikes, Captain?"

"You misunderstand me."

"We can be quite reasonable, Captain. As you well know. As reasonable as Toussaint and his black Jacobins, Captain."

"Surely the goal of an egalitarian community, of a stateless state is to be hoped for, where people will live in harmony and exploitation will wither away?"

"You are, with all your fierceness, Captain, or perhaps that passion is part of it, you are a romantic. A Christian romantic. This is my question: Are we to be made a shining example of the impossible? Or be treated as a group of living, breathing human beings?"

"Why impossible?"

"Why not allow us to be human?"

"So you see the profit motive as a measure of humanity."

"I would say instead self-sufficiency. Simple."

Annie, the Ethiopian Delineator, after a fruitless serenade of the gathered company, has turned as green as the baize on the billiard table, underneath his cork. His visage has a grayish pall to it. He lurches toward a porthole. I trust he knows which way the wind blows. Though in a storm such as this, the wind is never constant; it shifts always, suddenly.

Our conversation entered dangerous waters.

"It is my understanding, Captain, that the model for your stateless state is the Kingdom of God. Am I right?"

"Indeed, Mrs. Pleasant. That of which Jesus taught."

"Am I correct that the Kingdom of God is just that?"

"I don't follow."

"A realm, Captain, where a savior, lord, a King of Kings is crucial to the establishment?"

"Yes. Our Lord and Savior Jesus Christ."

"A theocracy, then?"

"A realm guided by the Son of God."

"Yes. The one and only."

"Please take care not to blaspheme, my friend."

"I cannot blaspheme that which I do not hold dear, Captain. You may be a Christian, and I do respect your version. Love and do what you will.

"But I have also witnessed the missions along the Camino Real, where Indian people are stacked one on top of the other in unmarked graves, in yards the size of an undertaker's anteroom. Thousands of them. Worked to death by the fathers, infected by the fathers."

"That is not Christianity, Mrs. Pleasant. That is the very thing I have fought my life against. The undermining of Christian ethics. The missions are evidence of the marriage between property and religion, with property taking the upper hand, as it usually does.

"Jesus has been used by the *padres*, and others, to shore up their enterprises, whether the genocide of the Indian or the Atlantic slave trade. His actual teaching could not be at a further remove from their practices."

"But usable by such as the fathers? the traders?"

"I imagine any philosophy can be made usable, can be usurped."

"But rather inconvenient for the likes of me. I do remember my Sunday school lessons here and there, in between Quasheba's teaching and my father's story-telling. First Corinthians, fifteen, verses twenty-two to twenty-three. I trust you know the words, Captain?"

" 'For as in Adam all die, so also in Christ shall all be made alive. But each in his own order: Christ the first fruits, then at his coming those who belong to Christ.' "

"And what if we don't belong, Captain? What then? Do we end up being fed to the dogs, like the Arawak?"

"Those are the words of Paul, not Jesus. He would turn no one away. Never."

"I dread the pacification of my people, Captain. I dread the notion of suffering into redemption. You can understand that, I know."

"I do understand."

"Very well, my dear friend. The future of the African

in this country, if you really want my opinion, will only bear fruit if and when we get our own. Banks, schools, real estate, printing presses, newspapers, grocery stores, et cetera, and partake fully in free enterprise. And when we get our own congressmen, senators, judges. Male and female. And by that I mean living, breathing race-proud people, not some 'thank-you-massa-for-smiling-upon-my-woolly-head-and-only-in-America-could-something-like-such-a-wonder-ful-thing-happen-and-I-did-it-by-the-sweat-of-my-brow-and-with-books-kindly-Miss-Anne-done-loaned-me-and-now-I-reap-what-I-sow-and-I'se-one-happy-darky-and-castration-don't-hurt-one-little-bit-and-I-get-to-keep-my-balls-in-this-here-jar-all-pickled-in-moonshine.'

"Pardon my crudeness, Captain, but no, thank you. It will do us no good at all to wait to ask for Miss Anne's hand. No good to take to the hills . . ."

"The choice was Kansas."

"Well, then, to squat outside of Wichita, on a piece of virgin prairie, in a circle in some ersatz Africanness, bleeding Kansas beneath us, living off fruits and berries and nuts like Kongo Transcendentalists. Neither—"

"You mock us."

"Only with love, Captain Brown. Always."

I paused before continuing, to make sure he heard. He lowered his eyes to his lap, and for a moment I contemplated his huge hands, folded there; had I hurt him?

I softened my voice.

"Neither will it do us any good, as some have suggested, as my own, exhausted father did, to take a boat back to Africa in search of home, as if a reverse passage can reverse history. The time has passed for all that. We are no longer African. We are New World people, and we built this blasted country from the ground up. We are part of its future, its fortunes.

"We belong in the here and now."

We went back and forth like that for a while longer, sometimes head-on, sometimes aslant.

In the end we were two people with love for each other. It was that simple. That much of a wonder. And while I did not agree with J. B.'s vision of the dark-skinned future, I never for a minute distrusted his love.

I have grown so weary of interrupted conversations. That is what death is. It breaks off words between people. It leaves you with a longing for one last talk, or two, or three. A chance to say, "I do love you. I always will."

I was down South when I heard they had hanged him. I spent the day, head down, left foot dragging, immersed in memory. Can you hear me? I said aloud.

When he was captured there was a piece of paper in his pocket, with my words on it. "The axe is laid at the foot of the tree. When the first blow is struck, there will be more money to help."

Not much of a farewell, but at least a promise.

In the end our conversations wafted into the ether, meaningless.

Meaningless but to me who repeats them over and over in my head.

Company.

Looking back, even with all I had witnessed, I realized I have underestimated the strength of the ideology which underlay the institution.

In Boston, before I caught the train to the steamer, I bought a copy of one of our newspapers.

L Y N C H I N G

was spread across four columns. A story ran inside, apparently unrelated to the headline. MAN AND HIS FAMILY STARVE TO DEATH WHILE WAITING FOR THE MILLENNIUM.

Will we all?

My pen seems to have run off with me, and my memory.

The Ethiopian Delineator is nowhere to be seen, no doubt collecting himself for the evening's performance.

May you sleep at the heart of a tender comrade.

with my love,
Mary Ellen.

She folded the paper into an envelope, sat back, and closed her eyes.

The Ethiopian Delineator has retreated to his cabin, indisposed, but the hologrammatical man is still with her, standing in a corner of the green saloon against a bank of signs, one which advertises

A MATTER OF TIME
New Adventures for the Forgetful
10 Easy Exercises
by Madame P. Rosetta,
Registered Practitioner of Mesmerism

The advertisement featured several testimonials to the madame's technique

"I am a new man, thanks to the Rosetta Process."
—CRAZY HORSE

"I remember nothing."
—SAAT-JEE, Venus Hottentot

among others.

"I am with you always," the hologrammatical man says softly in Mary Ellen Pleasant's direction, without a sound, about to take his leave.

But she has fallen asleep and does not get his words.

When she wakes she watches as the steamer draws close to the Vineyard. She realizes slowly that she has spent the night at this desk, alone, not alone.

On the island, on a dune, she is eleven, a girl waiting for her father's ship, with outstanding grades from the Free African School, she is eager, as any child, to show him how good she is, to make him proud.

The pinafored girl waves to the approaching steamer, thinking Captain Parsons is about to make landfall, and barrels marked XXX will be offloaded and their people set free.

There will be a big celebration, a clambake perhaps, with corn and potatoes and clams and lobsters packed in seaweed and steamed on hot rocks.

But the girl is mistaken.

The ship that approaches is a ferryboat carrying an indisposed Delineator, a crowd of Methodists desperate for revival, herself at the age of sixty, thinking, nothing was that long ago, everything seems like yesterday, tomorrow.

Mary Ellen Pleasant is standing at the rail, her left arm raised, she makes a long fluid motion toward the girl standing on the dune, who thinks Captain Parsons greets her.

Everything is here, and now.

IV

TENDER COMRADES

Allegorical Portraiture

Something compelled Clover Hooper back to the alley by Ford's Theatre the morning after she and her cousin Alice and their man, Patrick, had their initial encounter with the alley-dwelling woman who said her name was Scheherezade.

But when they arrived the alley was empty, and the alley dweller was gone, her only traces shards from her clay pot, apparently smashed in her departure, and the remains of her camp fire, long cold.

What had happened?

Alice and Patrick turned toward the street.

"I should have asked her to accompany us," Clover said, feeling foolish, unreal as soon as she said it. "Give me a moment, please," she asked, and they left her there.

She bent down and with her right hand chose a broken piece of the clay pot, and slid it into the pocket of her skirt, where it nestled against another souvenir, a stone from the sunken road at Antietam. A witness. Another she had not saved.

She closed her hand around them, joining them in her memory.

She had lied to the stranger. Of course she'd had nightmares from her visits to the state asylum with her father and her sister. Some she still remembered. But she could not relate these to a stranger. Her father was a good man.

She had been five years old when her mother died, shut away in a tuberculosis sanatorium. What difference was there between a place like that and the place where her father looked into the eyes of the insane?

To her childish mind, none.

What difference was there between women who drank from their chamber pots and her? She had once witnessed such a thing, rapt, until her father turned her eyes away.

Even then the visits did not stop.

What difference between them and her?

In her worst moments she feared none. No difference at all.

But this did not make for sisterhood.

It did not matter that a woman such as she, educated, privileged, with access to capital, could never end up in a place like that.

Accommodation would be made. She might even be kept at home. In a room where she would be force-fed to approximate a rounded, female figure. Maternal, feminine. Soft. She was not and it frightened her.

She was too angular, everyone had noticed. Her breasts were boyish. Her hips unconvincing.

And she was possessed of artistic pretensions.

No woman she.

The war to her was a blessed event.

She tried to keep it going as long as she could.

She found a way, through the Shaw Memorial Committee, and in her meetings with the sculptor Saint-Gaudens, whose commission she championed.

It was he who sculpted the monument on her grave in Rock Creek Cemetery.

11 April 1881

My dear Alice,

Henry and I received your invitation for Saturday next. Henry will be in Boston and is delighted to accept, but I am unable to attend. That should gladden some extra woman's heart.

While I regret not getting up to see you, my reason is cause for great excitement.

I am to travel to New York City this weekend to meet with Augustus Saint-Gaudens at his atelier. I have been asked by the Memorial Committee to inform him that he is our first choice to execute the monument.

Wish me luck.

my love,
Clover.

5 May 1881

Augustus Saint-Gaudens
16 Bleecker Street
Greenwich Village
New York City, New York
Dear Mr. Saint-Gaudens:

We are delighted to inform you that we will meet the terms outlined by you in yours of 28th April. Mrs. Adams will be traveling to New York City with the photographs, etc., you request, as well as a contract for your services.

Yours sincerely,
Joshua Smith, for the Committee

7 May 1881

My dear Ned,

I will arrive on the 7:06 from Washington, Tuesday, May 10. I will stay the night with you and catch the 8:52 to New York City the next morning. If you could have the photographs and the saddle ready I would appreciate it. I shall treat them as the treasures they are. I promise.

love,
Clover.

7 May 1881

Augustus Saint-Gaudens
16 Bleecker Street
Greenwich Village
New York City, New York
Dear Mr. Saint-Gaudens:

I trust this finds you well. As Mr. Joshua Smith has no doubt informed you, I will be descending on your atelier once more. My brother Ned, like our cousin, was also in charge of a regiment of Negro troops. While no photographs exist of the men of the 54th, as you requested, Ned has in his possession two large souvenir portraits taken of his men. I am an amateur photographer and took the pictures as the men departed to the War. They are not terribly sharp, but should do for your purposes.

In addition I shall be carrying with me on the train the saddle used by Shaw, which was returned to his family along with his other effects.

I shall be at the Hotel Lafayette on University Place as of May 11.

May I add my thanks that you have accepted the commission?

Yours,
Marian Adams

29 January 1883

Mr. Augustus Saint-Gaudens
16 Bleecker Street
Greenwich Village
New York City, New York
Dear Mr. Saint-Gaudens:

I am one of the survivors of the 54th Massachusetts
Regiment. I understand from Mr. Joshua Smith, chairman
of the committee and longtime friend of my family, that
you have no likeness of our regiment with which to work
on our memorial—rather, the Shaw Memorial, as it's being
called. I am twenty years older than I was back then, an
"old soldier" you might say, but my bones have not shifted
that much, although I have inherited my father's cloud of
white hair, with which you may be familiar.

I regret not having been in touch with you sooner, but
I have been out West, seeking my fortune, as the saying
goes.

It is important to me that my comrades be depicted
to a man, individually, and not as background to our beloved colonel.

I cannot tell you your business, of course, but I will
do all I can to assist you, should you so wish.

Yours sincerely,
Lewis Douglass,
fmr. sergeant Mass. 54th.

17 February 1883

Mr. Lewis Douglass
10 Elleston Street
Jamaica Plain,
Massachusetts
Dear Mr. Douglass:

I am sorry not to have responded to your letter of Jan. 29 prior to this. I am an untidy man, as most artists seem to be, and misplaced your letter to me. I thank you for your offer to assist me in my work on the monument. Should I have need of your help I will not hesitate to request it.

For your information, I am using live models at this stage of the process, which stage should continue for at least three more years. A tedious business. I select the models from the streets of New York for the most part, men in need of a few dollars. I know that the men of the 54th were of all ages and sizes and types, so I assure you I am careful to select a wide variety of men, to reflect the diversity of your comrades. I hope you will be pleased with the result. I am an Irishman, and so honor your caution with regard to becoming "background."

Thank you again,
Augustus Saint-Gaudens.

5 October 1883

My dear Alice,

We have just returned from Niagara Falls, where we tasted of the American Sublime. Standing there, I was dwarfed in her immensity, the spray creating a hundred rainbows. I stood at the edge of a rock ledge, against Henry's better judgment, I might add. No fear. I felt none. I only wanted to be enveloped in her hugeness, smothered in her power. I wish you could experience it.

my love,
Clover.

11 November 1883

Mr. Augustus St.-Gaudens
16 Bleecker Street
Greenwich Village
New York City, New York
Dear Augustus:

I am writing on behalf of my brother Ned, who has become anxious with regard to the two photographs of his regiment. They are practically his only memento of that time, and his only physical trace of the men in his command.

Since I was the author of them, and the one who suggested you use them in the Memorial, I feel obliged on Ned's behalf to ask you if and when you will be finished with them. I could easily catch a train anytime from Washington to New York City to retrieve them. Please let me know. And I hope I give you no inconvenience.

yours,
Marian Adams.

19 January 1884

Mrs. Henry Adams
1607 H Street
Washington, D.C.
Dear Marian:

Please have patience with me. I long ago decided, and should have informed you of this, to disregard the two photographs of your brother's regiment, in favor of portraits from the life. I find my models on the city streets, men with distinctive faces, some wearing pieces of uniforms, some not born until after the War. In any event they are giving life to the piece. They will stand out, of that I am certain, around and behind the colonel's likeness. I am terribly sorry that you did not receive the photographs. I must have returned them at least six months ago, maybe more.

I do think you will be pleased with the result, with the Memorial. I think I'm almost halfway there.

Yours,
Augustus Saint-Gaudens.

25 January 1884

Dear Ned,

What to do? Saint-Gaudens has written me that he had no use for my pictures, and so returned them "at least six months ago, maybe more." Well, you didn't receive them and I didn't receive them, so I guess some poltergeist or demon or some such spirited them away.

I feel responsible for their loss. Please forgive me.

Clover.

25 January 1884

Dear Ellen,

Why was it Papa never brought Ned along to the asylum when he took us there?

Clover.

27 January 1884

My dear Clover,

I received your rather monosyllabic note yesterday. I think the reason Ned was not brought along, or at least the reason given us, was that he was a boy and we were girls.

I do hope you are taking care of yourself.

Please. Give my regards to Henry.

love,
Ellen.

P.S. Yes, I realize it makes no sense whatsoever, but it's all I remember.

October 5, 1884

My dear Alice,

I hate to bother you with this; truly.

The old feeling is descending again. It becomes harder and harder to stay. I can only describe it as a sense of unreality, or unrealness. I feel of no substance. As if a shaft of light would pass right through my body, never casting a shadow from its contours. I am flimsy. I do not photograph well.

Saint-Gaudens wrote that my photographs of Ned's regiment must have been lost in transit, and that was some time ago. Still no pictures. I'm only sorry for Ned. To lose the faces of his tender comrades, no matter how poor the focus.

I'm past caring.

Henry tells me, if we had children.

Well, we don't. And I've even studied one of those dreadful books; it is in my bedstand and has succeeded only in confusing the issue.

There's a doctor here who specializes. I've refused.

I'm past forty. No hope.

You told me once of imagining you and me home-steading out West. I know you felt awkward in telling me. Embarrassed. You shouldn't have been. I have the need to move and I cannot. I am landlocked. With a husband any woman would give her right arm for.

Hurrah, hurrah.

He is a good man. I must not complain. He travels well. He appreciates a change of scene, as do I. He negoti-ates the casbah with as much grace as he negotiates Mont St. Michel.

I too have allowed myself the luxury of imagining. Of being swept across the Great Plains. Maybe being one of those itinerant photographers, the ones they call *shadow-catchers*. I remember that expression because I remember that woman in the alley; do you remember her? She asked me if I was "one of those shadow-catchers." No. I can't even catch my own shadow.

Oh, God, what is wrong with me? Make me real. You are all so real. Make me real too.

Clover.

October 12, 1884

My dear Clover,

I am in my room on what is a blustery and chill afternoon. The leaves fly everywhere, swirl outside my window. Down below, Patrick is attempting to gather them into burlap sacks, to little avail. There are schoolchildren downtown, celebrating the voyages of the great discoverer. At least that's what the papers have promised. I have not been downtown in God knows when.

Your letter of the 5th distressed me greatly. I only wish I could offer some comfort, something to ease your mind. You are so *real* to me. I remember the woman from the alley very well indeed. I remember your speaking of her on our trip to Antietam, and during the rest of our time in the capital. I caught the regret in your voice. Surely you could do no more.

Your ability to concern yourself, to care for the less fortunate, has always impressed me. You lend yourself to others.

My dear, I pray these feelings will pass, and that you know you are loved, by myself and by so many others, deservedly so.

Alice.

October 15, 1884

My dear Alice,

Thank you for trying to put my mind at rest. If you only knew how inadequate I feel, how I felt that day in Washington in that alley by Ford's Theatre. It amuses me that you think of me as lending myself to others. I wish I could.

I stare at photographs of myself, the only evidence at hand that I exist, am three-dimensional, and I can't recognize the subject. Who is she?

Her eyes are hooded, her head tilted at an angle which obscures her likeness. She remains hidden from sight, a secret. I compare these portraits with those I have taken of others and am astonished. The frankness of others. The way they look into the lens. Here I am. Catch me if you can.

Not I.

Was I afraid that she might touch me in turn?

Mary Ellen Pleasant eyes me in the portrait I made in 1858. Her left eyebrow snakes over a black-irised eye. I stand accused.

By myself? or her?

I dreamed last night I was in the bowl of space, on a beach in the Milky Way, surrounded by stars. I felt in the dream entirely at home, at peace. In dreamtime, with none of the old terror encroaching. To be consumed by light. To become light.

I was reading the letters of Marguerite de Navarre. She writes in one of keeping a deathwatch. She sat at the bedside of one of her ladies-in-waiting, trying to detect the exact moment the soul departed the body. She described the instant as almost imperceptible. The tiniest speck of light.

To be joined to the rest of the universe by light.

Clover.

March 8, 1885

My dear Clover,

The feelings you describe have long plagued our family, that you know. But they are manageable. It is perhaps the nature of certain thinking, feeling beings to suffer this melancholy. The price of existence in a sense. At least that is how I have dealt with my own melancholia. In answer to your question: no, absolutely not. Mama was sent away to a place in the country to treat her tuberculosis, but the doctors found she was a hopeless case. That's all that happened. She was not insane. She was not in the asylum. You must try to put these things out of your mind. If not for your own sake, think of Henry.

my love,
Ellen.

August 2, 1885

My dear Alice,

I am consumed by the mystery of it all. The mystery of the human absence. Moonrise. Niagara's thunder. Life on a planet spinning into the dark. It is my own peculiar form of consumption.

The doctor has suggested rest, cold baths. I have agreed to the former, have no use for the latter.

I think Henry understands.

I am lying here in the heat of a Washington summer, the dog days, on a bed at the top of the house. The room is dark, the shades are drawn.

I have an overwhelming desire to do the forbidden thing, to meet myself. I must not.

Clover.

September 17, 1885

Mrs. Henry Adams
1607 H Street
Washington, D.C.
Dear Marian:

Thank you for your note of August 17. In response to your question: Work on the Memorial goes well, but more slowly than I would like. I envision an unveiling no later than 1893, with luck. I have limited the design of the piece to portraits of sixteen soldiers, Negroes all, of course, in low relief, bayonets pointing up, marching in front and behind the Colonel, in much higher relief, on horseback. May I thank you, and your brother Ned, once again, for the loan of Shaw's saddle. I assure you I am taking the utmost care of it, having it soaped and rubbed religiously. I look

forward to the day when we sit together at the unveiling of
the work and I express my gratitude for all you have done
to make it possible.

Augustus.

November 11, 1885

My dear Clover,

The strangest creature came to visit the other day. Dr.
Mary Walker, she who passed as a man during the War and
tended the troops at the front. Apparently no one, officer
or enlisted, had a clue as to her femininity. She is quite
manly in her way, not in appearance but in demeanor.
Straightforward in her speech, gallant in her gestures. The
sort of woman who has no doubt about her purpose in life,
not unlike Mary Ellen Pleasant.

There is a movement to secure for her—Dr. Walker,
that is—the Congressional Medal of Honor in recognition
of her valorous conduct under fire. She'd come for my
support, which I of course gave freely. I had tea brought up,
introduced the doctor to Atthis—I am trying to make you
smile—and we talked for a few hours. In exchange for my
support she told me all about her experiences in the theater
of war. "My dear," she said, "I doubt they would have
turned me away had they found out. Such was their need.
I became quite adept at amputation, particularly of legs.
The limbs were stacked like cordwood after some encoun-
ters. Old and young, but mostly young, of course, scrawny,

muscled, bowed, in all as different and as similar as tree limbs. I tried to cut as cleanly as I could, but had to work in haste, often as darkness was falling, and the rate of infection was dreadful. I will spare you any more detail."

She is quite tiny; one wonders at the strength necessary to cut a man's leg from his body, or a boy's. "All in the wrist, my dear," she said, as if reading my mind. She held her hands out for me to examine. "And the rhythm of the saw."

Ye gods. That brings it home. I shall always think of her as "sawbones."

My dear, I hope you are feeling better, more composed, and that you get to Boston sometime soon.

My love to you, regards to Henry.

Alice.

November 24, 1885

My dear Alice,

I suppose, in answer to your hope, I am more composed. I actually went riding the other day near Arlington.

I wonder that you refer to Dr. Walker as a strange creature. Why is that, do you think? Is it because her hands are not trained for women's work? Neither are mine. Am I then strange to you?

Because of her gallantry? I wonder.

I am attempting to transform this "sickroom" into a darkroom. I went to an exhibit at the National Museum a week ago, a display by the man who has developed a new process for printing photographs from negatives. His name is Siebert and he owns the patent. I shall pay him a fee so that I may use it.

I have a need to record my country.

"Out of the cradle endlessly rocking,"

Clover.

A Letter of Condolence

14 June 1886

Henry Adams
c/o The American Consul
Papeete,
Tahiti
Dear Henry Adams:

Forgive the lateness of these greetings.

This letter has had the devil's own time catching up to you, if in fact it has.

Never have I seen so many exotic postmarks, on each return to me the letter has been embossed anew. Fiji. East Timor. Tonga. Bougainville. Java. Each with the imprimatur of a mother state.

My, my.

The letter and its envelope barely hold together at this point, so I am writing it over again.

The circuitous route began when the letter was re-jected at your address in Georgetown, and returned to me with a note from your secretary, informing me of your intent to circumnavigate the globe.

It seems we are playing hide-and-seek in Polynesia.

Believe me, I understand the necessity of your travels, given the circumstances of your great loss.

In any case, futile though this exercise be, I do hope you receive my message of condolence sooner rather than later.

If this is returned once again I shall attempt a note in a bottle.

And with this tedious preface I suddenly realize I am writing to a man I have never met, about a loss as intimate as can be.

But you may have heard of me through your wife, Clover, as I have heard of you.

Your *late* wife, I find I must say, an amendment which appalls me, as I am sure it does you.

Please accept my deepest sympathy.

I was indeed greatly dismayed and saddened to read of her death in the San Francisco papers. "Paralysis of the heart" was the first report, until some enterprising journal-ist unraveled what I gather was the actual situation of her death. How painful for you. How unnecessary! I refer to the reportage, of course.

Then, some idiot—he couldn't be anything else—cited the cause of Mrs. Adams's suicide as "failure to become popular." Why not failure of her hair to curl, her eyes to twinkle, her skin to remain girlish? Am I telling you anything new? Or did our benighted reporter take his cues from the eastern papers, as we in the West do far too often, to our detriment?

Clover and I met one evening in Boston, at a gathering where Frederick Douglass spoke of his recent trip to Ireland, and the living conditions of the Irish poor. He described what he believed was the natural alliance between the Boston Irish, kin of the people he had visited, and the Africans beginning to cluster in the city. It was an alliance of great potential, he said, not yet made actual—I remember his words clearly. One thing stood in its way. And this, he said, broke his heart.

The evening floods back at me. But a political memory has no place in a letter of condolence. Does it?

Clover and I happened to be seated next to one another, and chatted briefly during the intermission between Douglass's speech and the question-and-answer period. She asked to take my photograph, and that was the occasion of our next meeting.

I took the train out to her father's residence, where she then lived. The year was 1858. I was in Boston on business. She greeted me at the gate, the reins of her horse, Powhatan, in one hand, the other extended in greeting. She had it in her mind to photograph me astride the animal. I asked her why. She responded shyly, as if my asking had upset her. I was glad I hadn't questioned the horse's name, which to be honest bothered me.

"I have heard of your work through the grapevine,"

she said by way of explaining, almost whispering. "I
thought an equestrian pose fitting."

At that time my work was not to be spoken of, to
protect a certain enterprise, to protect myself. It is not
spoken of now for other reasons, but no need to go into
that.

I asked her what she knew, and how she had come to
know it.

"I have heard you are a conspirator for freedom," she
said.

"Forget anything you have ever heard about me," I
said, rather sharply. "But I must know who it was that told
you. Our work is not the stuff of gossip."

She seemed to take several steps back, and to hood her
eyes with one hand so there was no engaging them. "I am
sorry," she said. "I do not remember the source. I promise
to tell you if I recall. Really."

I let her demurral pass, and suggested she photograph
me under the rose trellis at one side of the house.

She was quite young, her life one of privilege. Her
mistake was an honest, if unfortunate, one.

I repeated these things to myself as I sat there, amused
at the picture of me as an icon on horseback, the shadows
of the rambling roses climbing across me, thorns and all.

She went about her picture taking artfully, silently.

Afterward, I thought our earlier exchange behind us,
but there was a reticence about her; she acted as if I had
reprimanded her, and of course I had. One had to be on
guard at all times, those days. For saboteurs, for romantics,
which is what I judged Clover to be, rightly or wrongly.

When I received the picture, it was accompanied by a thank-you letter, and a reiteration of her promise not to tell anyone anything about me.

That is the memory of your wife I wish to offer you, along with my condolences. The portrait she made of me is really quite good. She allowed me to see the fierceness some complain about, others celebrate, which I never took very seriously. Not that the fires have been tamped, not at all.

That thing, that Frederick Douglass said caused his heart to break, may be the death of us all. But what has that to do with a letter of condolence, may I ask?

Nothing at all.

I have heard that coconut milk does wonders for a broken heart.

Yours,
Mary Ellen Pleasant

On December 6, 1885, Clover Adams drank the potassium cyanide she used in developing her pictures. Her last months were marked by a frenzy of work. She is buried near soldiers in Washington, D.C. Saint-Gaudens was the author of her monument.

A figure, modeled from the life, both male and female, whose eyes are shrouded.

The Shaw Memorial was unveiled on Memorial Day, 1897. The procession to the unveiling was led by surviving members of the 54th Massachusetts Regiment. Booker T. Washington and William James sat side by side on the reviewing stand. Washington gave a powerful address.

Alice Hooper also passed on. The painting by J.M.W. Turner, *Slavers Throwing Overboard the Dead and Dying, Typhon Coming On,* went in 1899 to the Boston Museum of Fine Arts, where it hangs today. Go see it. Take the kids.

Company

"A body needs company." Truer words had never been written, and Annie knew it, although her nature took her to the other side, as inexorable as a riptide, and Mary Ellen knew it.

But even for Annie the solitude could get to be too much, and when it did, and the bottle trees threatened to speak in tongues, to get the spirit, or to wear hoods, to garland themselves with lengths of rope, when she felt herself surrounded, she walked to her captive company, and partook of storytelling, even as those in charge pressed Bingo! on the group.

Between her solitude and her community, were visits from Rachel DeSouza, #11246, late of the synagogue in the density of the South American jungle, whose last impression, the thing that would come into focus were she to press her fingertips against her eyelids, was a *mikva*, on the edge of which a lizard, wearing an impossibly defiant green, sunned herself.

Rachel was the only colonist Annie knew outside the fences, and Rachel chose her appearances carefully, so Annie looked forward to her, and she would be welcomed.

Rachel had arrived at Carville sometime ago, with a Surinamese strain of the disease considered particularly dangerous. It had been assumed by the pathologists and diagnosticians that her long association with the Surinamese Maroons, the Bush Negers, incubated her particular form of plague.

She shrugged. What did she know? Her company of like-minded rebels, all focused on one thing, the cessation of the Trade, had all seemed sound.

Her version of plague was especially dangerous, the doctors said, because it was silent. That is, no outward signs were apparent: no toe drops, or finger drops, no flat place where a nose should have been, no missing lips. The damage raged, the scientists told her, on the inside.

On the inside, they said, invisible to the naked eye, you are falling apart. Scar tissue is building up.

Yet she felt fine.

She could not, they insisted. Papers had been written, samples of infected organs floated in glass jars. All reached the same conclusion: The Surinamese strain flourished especially among Jews and Maroons.

Against their scientific delight, their curiosity and fear, Rachel made herself scarce. She felt fine.

Soon after her arrival, Rachel found a way of eluding

the keepers, managing to slip through a break in the fence, stealing away for hours at a time. She usually made her break during the weekly confession, when she, as the only Jew (at least no other had come forward), was more, at least felt more, conspicuous than ever in the Catholic domain.

The *marranos,* from whom she descended, had at least each other; company again. Company in their hiding places, guerrilla bands, in the prisons, in the processions, on the ships of Colón and Magellan, across the seven seas, contradicting the flatness of the Earth—were it round, would Jews be safer?—in the thick undergrowth of the New World.

The time through which her people lived, and died, raged in her bones, was witnessed in her dreams. You can't imagine the chaos, the people running, the fires burning for days and nights on end. By their light family treasures were buried, only to be unearthed and tossed on the bonfires, unless the inquisitors could make use of them, melt them down, alter them to a new purpose. By their light the bones of the mother of Juan Luis Vives (great Christian humanist and crypto-Jew) were exhumed, and tossed into unhallowed ground.

Some among her people thought the sand on the floor of the synagogue was a reference to the day when they would be as many as there was sand on the shore.

These were the optimists.

Among the Maroons she had company. Some her own, some not.

·   ·   ·

For confession at the colony a priest came down the Mississippi from a neighboring parish, a man who insisted on
draping purple velvet over the confessional grille to impede
transmission of the disease, succeeding only in making
confession difficult, obstructing both admission and pen-
ance.

No one suggested an *auto da fé*, but Rachel felt the
eyes of the *religieuses* on her, burning as she bent over the
vegetable garden she tended, their beads clicking past her
on the stone paths. In silence she worked, not daring even
to sing to herself.

She saved her voice for the story-telling, for visits to
Annie.

Once she broke her rule and said, "Did you know,
sisters, that Sor Juana Inés de la Cruz, la Decima Musa, first
genius of the New World, was a Jew?" But she kept her
voice so soft even she could not hear.

Rachel, for one, was grateful when the United States Public
Health Service took the place over.

Rachel approached Annie's house this afternoon as she
always did, even at this advanced age. From the river, tying
her rowboat, one she had rescued from the shallows and
mended, to the stump of a live oak tree. A mother alligator
lolled nearby, her tiny offspring sleeping on her back.

The letters on the bow of the boat spelled BEN-
DIGAMOS, from the old Sephardic song she remembered.
Bendigamos en el Altisimo it began, Let us bless the High-

est / For bread, first of all, then *Dios bendiga la Casa esta / Que nunca falta en elle fiesta,* God bless this House / That it may never be without rejoicing, *Tarde ni manana ni siesta a nos / Y a todos Hijos de Israel,* Evening or morning or afternoon, for us / And for all the Children of Israel, *Amen-ve-Amen,* Amen and Amen.

She had but to recall the first blessing and the words came flooding back to her from the synagogue in the jungle and she could see the *mikva,* the lizard in her impossible green posing like an odalisque.

Surrounding her was another jungle, with Annie's dwelling, it could not be called a home, strung with escaped, ruinate green, gray-green, blue-green, river-nourished green.

This lone visitor entered through a tunnel of green into a cave of green, her passages announced by the clink and hum of the bottles in communion with the breezes.

Annie's hiding place, that was it, her hideout.

Annie was perched on an upended wooden crate, its stickered end advertising NATIVE LOVE, which image was captured by a feathered man and a feathered woman and some Georgia peaches. She was busy with something in her lap, which her hands worked over and over. A metal strongbox, rust gathering at the hinges, was to her right on the floor of the sloping porch, a pile of stuff was at her left.

"Miss Annie," Rachel greeted her, her hand sweeping upward and across, her words caught by the bottles so that the visitor was accompanied by a chorus of echoes and a-mens.

Annie looked up from her business, peering over her spectacles into the almost impenetrable green.

"Ah, it's you, Miss Rachel," she said, as if there could have been someone else. "It is good to see you." And so it was. So many souls had passed through her life, in and out. Now she was down to one.

"Have I caught you at a bad time? You seem occupied."

"Not at all. I'm just going over some old trash, letters, souvenirs. You know. Time to clear these things out, I think."

"You don't sound very certain."

"Well, the time has come."

"Don't be rash, old friend. I for one know about lost things. Don't discard memory, or that which instigates it."

"My memory often fails to be instigated, as you put it. I can't even remember who the people in this picture were, or how I might be connected to them, and yet here I am, in the middle of them." She held up a dented tintype in which a group in Sunday dress, so it seemed, or special-occasion costume, were arranged on a palm-bordered lawn, females in front, the males a phalanx behind them. The figure who was Annie, a child, sitting cross-legged in the foreground. The ghost of a peacock walked out of the frame.

"Of course, they must have been connected to me, family. They are *gens inconnu* by the looks of them, and all *gens inconnu* are related. I wonder what the occasion was, the day of the week, the food that was served. I can guess at the year, if that indeed is my likeness. Oh, well." She discarded the picture in the pile at her left.

"Do you prefer I leave you be?" Rachel asked.

"No. I could use the company. Forgive me, I don't mean *use*. I am glad to see you; I am glad that you came. I salute the seaworthiness of *Bendigamos*, your strength." She smiled, paused. "Have you heard the news from Atlanta?"

How could the woman bear the heaviness in the air? Rachel wondered.

The overgrowth of the landscape smothered.

The air was made of water.

Unbreathable.

Undrinkable.

Had she heard anything? She was trying to remember what she had heard.

Suddenly she was trying to catch her breath.

Finally she said: "The priest brought news today. This morning. He made a general announcement to all of us gathered in the chapel. The head nurse called our numbers, one by one, and one by one we filed in."

"And?"

"And what you and I decided was the inevitable happened. As much as we chafe against our instincts, our sense of humanity, the inhumane."

"What did the priest say exactly?"

"He began by casting the sign of the cross over us, filling his mouth with holy water and spewing it in a circle at his feet, to ward us off, I imagine; his terror of infection is always apparent. He cleared his throat and spoke finally. 'The Sodomite who violated Mary Phagan has gotten his just deserts.' That's what he said."

"Dear God."

"Yes. He was not finished. 'Let us pray for his soul,' he instructed us. Some did."

"That bastard."

"You might say that. There he was, bringing the good news to the entombed. No doubt we too have gotten our just deserts."

"What else did he say?"

"Oh, he gave a lot of details. He is, as he reminded us, well placed in the priestly community."

"Tell me. I want to know what he told you. What you heard."

Rachel took a deep breath, and still found the air wanting. There were so many stories inside her. She had been listening to them, experiencing them, telling them back, and even in the telling was not free of them. She turned her dark eyes on Annie's light ones.

"I'll try. The air is so close; how can you bear it?"

"Takes me home. Please."

"Each night a crowd lined the streets of Atlanta, he said. Almost festive, he said. Chanting 'Hang the Jew,' he said. It was only a matter of time, he said, before the majority ruled."

"In the name of all that's holy."

"Yes. He offered analogies, not the ones I would have chosen, needless to say. I think we can skip those."

"What else?"

"Can you imagine the scene on Peachtree Street?"

"I have seen mobs in my day."

"As have I. Granada in fourteen-ninety-two was quite festive. As was Cadiz, Salamanca. An abundance of torchlight, broken glass, horses racing with the madness of the *palio.*"

"A holiday atmosphere?"

"Oh, yes. In Atlanta a holiday, an exorcism complete with iced tea and shortcake."

"And hoods, of course."

"Not just. Ladies decked out in their best clothes. Stays in place. Hair piled high. Lace collars nice and tight. Bankers in their three-piece suits, watch fobs shiny across their pot bellies.

"Tell me something," Rachel interrupted herself, "Why do men of that ilk refer to their pot bellies as corporations? I've always wondered."

"Something to do with corporeal, I imagine. Or prosperity."

"Yes. But let me finish. The street was lined with children. Everybody's children, fat cheeks rosied against the burning cross, even the sick children take on an aura of health."

"Except the Jews' children," Annie assisted.

"Yes. They were in safekeeping."

"Time to time people pass by here, usually in the evening, a blur of white, or sometimes distinct by the light of the moon. Sometimes you can smell the tar, see the flames dance into the night sky."

"I wonder what was said in the churches; what the schoolteachers taught. Did they write Leo Frank across the blackboard?"

"Would you have a drink?"

"Oh, yes. Please."

"A bottle of cognac Mary Ellen sent one October, I don't recall the year."

Annie poured the liquor and handed Rachel a glass.

"I find it harder and harder to keep track of events, of how things fit into time. Even with this box of things. Especially with this box of things. What happened? When? Who do these faces belong to? Did I love them? What was the occasion?"

Annie fingered the ridges in the dented tintype. "What became of them?"

"I wonder what will become of his wife?"

"I imagine she will disappear. Into thin air, as the magicians say."

"I find myself trying to be with him at the last."

From the mists over the river came the cry of a turtle.

"Look at this. My, my." Annie sighed. "I have not seen this in donkey's years. I had forgotten all about it. But I recognize it."

"What?"

"This." She held up a square of cloth for Rachel to see. "This goes way, way back." She spread the patch of appliquéd cotton across her lap.

"A keepsake from before the war. Someone made it for me."

The patch was discolored, with traces of mildew at the edges. The places where it had been folded over on itself were indelible lines by now, crevices obscuring the original image. Only with imagination could you draw it out.

"Can you see it?" Annie asked.

"I'm not sure."

"I probably can because I once memorized it."

"Well, what is it?"

"A lion with a rifle. Now can you make it out?"

The rifle was represented by a long, thin swatch of red silk, now faded, snipped from a lady's—daring, possibly French—petticoat, or a gentleman's four-in-hand. This image was attached to the background by XXXXX's of cross-stitchery, crosses breaking off here and there.

The hammer, the trigger of the gun were chain-stitched with black carpet thread; gaining darkness against the faded silk, they were unmistakable.

The gun was carried by a lion. His gaze dominated the piece once your eyes settled on it. Teeth were bared, long and ivory, cut from an antebellum tablecloth or dinner napkin. Eyes were obsidian buttons, arced by woollen eyebrows. A black velvet tongue unfurled from a golden mouth.

The mane had thinned a bit, but enough remained to suggest a lion's majesty.

"A warrior's portrait, African-style," Annie said.

"You?"

"Once, perhaps. Yes, once."

"And who was the artist?"

"A man in South Carolina, a house slave who worked

as a butler. He inherited his mother's scrap bag. Piecing cloth together was his passion. She had been collecting for years, stealing, scrounging, keeping her eyes open. She passed it all on to him. He was not above a little thievery, not at all, to keep himself in scraps, to keep the legacy going.

"He carried a small razor at all times. He could slice a piece of cloth from a guest's cloak while helping the gentleman into it."

"Gracious."

"Yes. This patch was part of a larger piece. I should say was intended to become part of a larger piece. We were to commemorate ourselves. Like the Bayeux tapestry. I am only being slightly ironic."

"I can tell."

"There were men and women like Barabbas, that was his name, all throughout the country, snipping scraps from linen closets, nurseries, ladies' boudoirs, hope chests.

"In the end, of course, it did not happen. No. Our historical moment was lost, so our tapestry is dissembled. Oh, it exists piece by piece. Some pieces have been buried with those who have passed on. Some are forgotten, misplaced. Some may line jewelry boxes, gather dust in attics, be used as shoeshine rags. Who knows?"

"Tell me what did not happen."

"You've asked me that before. I've told you: Everything did not happen.

"Everything.

"What did not happen, you ask? All I know is I was captured. Some were killed. Died in action. Were hanged under the law. Some escaped back to Canada. Mary Ellen managed to escape, barely, found her way back to San Francisco. John Brown is written down in the history books as a madman, fanatic, whose last sentient act on the way to the gallows was to kiss a black baby; none of which is true."

"There was the war at least."

"Yes. But it wasn't the same; you know that. There is a chasm between the war and what we planned."

Rachel nodded and sipped from the blood-red snifter.

"All I know is we were dispatched South, most of us driving wagons loaded with guns and ammunition, concealed under other goods. One woman was supposedly an itinerant midwife. Her rifles were concealed under lying-in blankets, bouquets of dried herbs, brewed to ease birth pangs, tins of aloe vera, used to make nipples supple. Were she stopped, she was to say she was on her way to a certain plantation where there were an inordinate number of lying-in deaths, of mother and child. You see, we were quite thorough.

"And we knew we could count on the suicide and infanticide of slave women . . . it was happening all the time.

"I was a dark-skinned man, a transformation obtained with a magic elixir, one endorsed by preeminent minstrels. The empty bottle hangs on that tree yonder. Another souvenir, like the cloth. I carried forged papers and a revolver inside the breast of my overalls. We all had forged papers. They'd been drawn up in Canada under the auspices of Mary Shadd Carey, in the colored schoolhouse.

"Some papers declared us free. Others said, 'Please

allow my slave Hezekiah, Goliath, Holofernes, Queen of Sheba, whomsoever, to pass. He-she-it is on an errand, et cetera, signed Massa whatsoever.' Things like that. We might have been a troupe of traveling players.

"Mary Ellen passed herself off as a blacksmith. She was truly something. She dressed as a house servant in San Francisco, came to the convention in Chatham dressed as a jockey, went South as a blacksmith, finally escaped as a middle-aged woman of African-American descent, which she was. Disguise was something she knew well. We all did. It was practically my birthright; you know that. Disguise. Masks. Never give out what you're thinking. The cane cutter in the iron mask, belled around the neck. The tribal story-teller taking on the face of each whose tale he tells. Disguise. How to pass through the nets. Like your own people. In search of a New World. We went South that way, to seek rebellion. Our plan was very simple. Arm the slaves.

"I was stopped a few times. I managed to deceive the patrollers for the most part. I was a cooper, did I tell you that? The samples of my skill were piled in the wagon behind me, on top of the guns.

"I was forced to kill. Twice. It was nothing, really. Well, not nothing. But I was surprised I felt so little.

"I was surprised I felt so little given the fact they were women. I was dressed as a man, as I said. It was Indian summer. A warm Indian summer afternoon. There was the softest breeze. The leaves were becoming golden, crimson. I stopped the wagon, tied the horse to a branch at the side of the road, and proceeded to look for a place to water her. She was hauling a hell of a load, and it was warm. I went into the woods with a bucket to fetch water for her, or to see if there was access to a body of water where she might take her fill. I walked for a while into deep woods and came into a clearing where I saw a small pond. I noticed two heads at the far end of the water, about a hundred yards away. Like I said, I wore overalls, and I had on a wide-brimmed hat, with my hair tucked inside, and my skin was dark.

"They could not leave me be. Two white women, naked. Immediately they saw me they began to scream. Jesus, what a racket! I was terrified. I was quite deep in a woods I did not know. Was their home nearby? Husbands? Fathers? I came closer to try to calm them, but knew that was no use. I couldn't run, they'd have had a posse out after me within the hour. I think I knew in my heart that as soon as they began their pathetic, but dangerous, terror, the die was cast.

"I fired once over their heads, more to get myself used to the task ahead than anything, then I shot each of them. The screaming stopped, and they sank under the water, some air bubbles in their wake. It was finished.

"I had killed two unarmed women, except they weren't.

"Do you understand?"

Rachel nodded.

"After I shot the first one, in the instant before I shot the second our eyes met. She stared, silent. Stunned. As if being shot by an African man, a slave as far as she knew, was the last thing she expected; it no doubt was.

"I stood there for a few minutes trying to take in what I had just done. Quiet was all around me. No sound of men coming to the aid of womanhood. Thank God. I filled the mare's bucket and went on my way. I kept waiting to be horrified; I was not.

"The day of insurrection was to have been November 2, 1859. We would be well set, having made contact with our people in the quarters some time before. We couldn't give anyone that exact date. Spies were everywhere, some in our own skins. But not as many as some books might have it. People were forewarned something was about to happen. The plans for arson were in place, the poisoners ready. There was a new kind of silence. We were all waiting.

"I was on the road leading from Charlottesville, on my way toward Monticello, when the silence gave way to noise, and I was told the news. An old woman approached me on the road: 'It is finished,' she said, our code for failure. She walked on. I found it hard to take in. But eventually did, by repeating the phrase over and over. I managed to break for the Maroon encampment in the Blue Ridge Mountains. Safe. I took a breath. Spoke with comrades, as we tried to figure out what the hell had gone wrong.

"In a few days we were raided. The women in the camp, Indians and Africans, were killed before our eyes. I, with my blackened skin and in my masculine state, was chained to other men, on a gang. We were judged useful. We were marched down the mountain through an avenue of hanging women, and we all wept. At first my masculine state protected me. But eventually my sex became known.

"My sex became known . . ." she repeated.

"And Mary Ellen?" Annie asked, then answered. "Mary Ellen was in the Deep South when the guns went off. But she managed to work her way back North, and book passage on a steamship going around the Horn to San Francisco. At the gangplank she offered a white woman her first-class cabin for the woman's steerage passage; the woman agreed to the deal. Mary Ellen told the woman she hadn't realized colored couldn't travel first-class, so would the woman, apparently a new immigrant from Naples, do her a favor? *Prego?* All was well. The immigrant shook her head in wonder at the ways of the New World, but agreed.

"When they found Captain Brown after Harper's Ferry, they found a note from her in his pocket: 'The axe is laid at the foot of the tree. When the first blow is struck, there will be more money to help.' It was signed M.E.P., but her handwriting bought her some time, since her *M* looked more like a *W.* Of course, they did not seek the likes of her, someone they called Mammy Pleasant. They were looking for young white men, not a forty-eight-year-old black woman.

"Still, she could take no chances. Soon enough she was back in San Francisco, stirring up things for the city fathers, making money for the Cause.

"That's where we went our separate ways. She kept the faith, kept on pushing. I withdrew. Our differences were born of several things. She had promised her husband, right before he died, that she would use his money—he'd made a fortune investing in the China trade—and make more in her own enterprises, solely for the purpose of furthering the race. That she did. She was, as you no doubt have concluded, a woman of her word.

"I had come to this country, and this cause, seeking my own redemption, which was a selfish motive. Of course, I believed in destroying the Institution, but I put myself first.

"Mary Ellen forced the integration of public facilities in California, bringing a lawsuit against a cable car company. She, using connections in the state house, knowing where the bodies were buried, got legislation through which gave people of African descent the right to testify against people of European descent, and so forth.

"She was a liberator by marriage, and by inheritance. I on the other hand walked by myself, out of the place in which I was raised, and across a foreign landscape where, in my mother's words, I should not business, just as I should not have intercourse with lepers.

"Mary Ellen's mother provided her with a firearm.

"Ah, me. Are you bored to death by now?"

Rachel shot Annie a glance, impatient.

"Okay," Annie responded.

"Did you see her again?"

"Mary Ellen? My mother?"

"Mary Ellen."

"No. She wrote and asked me to come visit her. I think she wanted me to join her in the Cause, but I was finished. I know she wanted me to join her. Her energy, her refusal to give it up, even though she once preached it to me, was remarkable. She kept in touch off and on over the years. I have her letters somewhere in here." Annie gestured to the strongbox.

"Do you think ill of me? I wouldn't blame you if you did."

"I don't."

"But you were in someone else's fight and stood fast."

"There is no 'someone else's fight,' Annie, you know that."

"Now perhaps. Not then. I don't think I did."

"What would have made it yours?"

"On my island, burning the great houses to the ground, under my mother's nose, my father's hegemony."

"You sound like an angry child."

"Maybe."

"May I see her letters?"

"Please yourself." Annie hefted the strongbox over to where Rachel sat.

"What on God's green earth is this?" Rachel held up a shiny object which had been acting as a paperweight for a stack of yellowing sheets.

"Oh, that," Annie responded. "Speaking of Mamá . . ."

"Hers?"

"Not quite. This"—Annie took the small box from Rachel's hand—"this, my dear, was the subject of many a dinner table conversation way back then. Trotted out whenever there was a lull . . ."

"What is it exactly?"

"A snuffbox, but not just any snuffbox. One given my grandfather on my father's side by the Duke of Wellington, to commemorate the battle of Waterloo. He was, as family history tells it, the duke's aide-de-camp. My mother, his daughter-in-law, detested him, as he detested her. There was a crystalline fury between them. The usual reason: He thought his son had married down.

"She slid the snuffbox out of his coffin one hot night, as he lay in state in the rotunda of King's House. A very hot night and our funeral techniques left a great deal to be desired. No one remembered mummification. We had no such thing as refrigeration. All our preserving was done with salt. But even salted, he stank, quite high. The men posted at the corners of his catafalque tied silk squares over their noses and mouths. They looked like bandits.

"My mother was the bandit. She, brave, acquisitive thing, slid her hand—gloved, of course—into the mahogany box, and slid the snuffbox out, only briefly engaging the rotting old man. It was the least he owed her, she said, with such menace in her voice I wondered if he had claimed the right of *jus primae noctis* all those years ago; it was not unheard of. Some things European made the voyage to the New World intact. As you well know.

"But I did not ask.

"I did ask how she fooled the guards, and she said she begged for privacy, for one final kiss.

"She had nothing to lose, she said, with regard to her theft. If the box was found to be missing, a servant would of course get the blame, or one of the guards. Luckily for each no one noticed when they sealed the coffin. The old man had so many bijoux and bibelots, what with medals and crests and a plume here and there and a ring or two or three with seal and signet, and his sash designating him founder of the order of *gens inconnu.* He was a decorated man. Who would miss one more object?

"He would, of course, but he was dead. So the snuff-box came to me after being plucked from the jaws of death by my mother. I found it among my belongings after I had left the island. She'd wrapped it in a piece of kente cloth and left it there as a souvenir. Don't forget where you came from, *ma chère.* Who your people are. I can almost hear her."

"The things other things abide by," Rachel said. "I mean that thing, that box against your warrior's portrait."

"Yes. Like me."

"But you are wrong to say you have given it up, gave it up. Your heart has not abandoned it. I cannot believe that."

"As I was saying, not just any snuffbox, bought on a stroll along Jermyn Street or Piccadilly," Annie said, uncomfortable with Rachel's endorsement. She held the object at arm's length toward Rachel.

Rachel looked closer at it, and could detect what she assumed were the traces of a family coat-of-arms, but, like the appliquéd cloth, time had tampered with the detail.

"Here," Annie said. "Take it."

Rachel weighed the thing in her hands. "It's heavier than it appears."

Up close a fanciful beast, griffin or chimera, could be detected, faintly etched in the surface.

"Cut from the Rock of Gibraltar, my dear. Imagine. One of the Pillars of Hercules."

"Some of us came through Gibraltar," Rachel said. "The place is riddled with caves, fortresses, used by the Moors against the Spanish. Monkeys screaming all over the place. My people hid out there until they could go elsewhere."

"Sometimes I think you were back there yourself. At the Expulsion, I mean."

"I might well have been."

"The casual way they chip at the world. Excavate and mine and dig."

"I have this extraordinary memory of running. Running and running, and being chased. A common enough thing, I suppose, but I am running down a steep hill, toward a ship about to set sail. The ship raises the flag of Los Reyes Católicos. I must decide whether to board. I have no choice.

"Probably not a memory at all; the remnant of a bedtime story. My grandmother was quite the story-teller."

"I think we carry more within us than we can ever imagine. If bone structure is passed on, why not memory?"

"And this?" Rachel pointed to some faded words, next to the faded beast on the surface of the snuffbox.

"A bit of heraldry. My family's motto. *In hoc signo vinces. Arbeit macht frei. Honi soit qui mal y pense.* Take your pick. They all add up to the same thing."

"Which one exactly?"

"Truth to tell, I forget."

"Shall you ever return?"

"Shall you?"

"To where, may I ask? The place I came from is gone now."

"To visit the graves, I imagine."

"I wish to make a toast," Annie said after pouring each some more cognac.

"Please do."

Each woman raised her glass.

"I give you the beloved memory of Mary Ellen Pleasant."

"The beloved memory of Mary Ellen Pleasant," Rachel a-mened.

"Dedicated fighter in the Cause, Mother of Freedom, Warrior and Entrepreneur, who some believed came back from the dead in nineteen and six to avenge her good name, and the loss of property she suffered at the hands of the fathers of San Francisco, who finally brought her down, charging she was a witch, casting spells with her one blue eye and her one black eye, poisoning the city water supply, wreaking havoc at the stock exchange, souring the milk of nursing mothers.

"Was it not she? people asked. How else would you explain that after the fires, which raged for days, after the fires were finally put out, the only things left standing on Octavia Street were the eucalyptus trees she had planted herself?

"All the more remarkable since all over the city eucalyptus trees were exploding, incinerating themselves and their surroundings.

"Hers stood, as cool as she was.

"And the story grows. They say the magnificent quake was centered underneath what once had been her mansion, and that her initials were burned into the trunk of each of her trees, M.E.P., the *M* formed like a *W*."

"We can but hope," Rachel said.

They touched glasses.

First came the huge roar. An enormous sound. Not from above, but from beneath. Not a heavenly racket, like thunder. A thundering under the earth. At the tail end of the thunder came the movement. The pavements rolled. Streets cracked. Split.

It was 5:00 A.M. on the 18th of April, 1906. The shaking lasted one full minute, maybe more. Time which was elastic.

The U.S. Mint split apart and spit thousands of coins down its marble staircases, out its doors, into the streets. Then the streets of San Francisco, at least a few, were paved with gold.

The water mains broke. Water poured down the hills, gathered in the flats, flooding the Mission District, running into the China Basin and the bay.

At the Pacific Steamship Company, on the docks, the holding pen for immigrant Chinese, the movement cracked the walls and the place opened, and men who had been considering suicide ran through the streets.

A slave woman, kept in a crib since her arrival on Gold Mountain six years before, gazed more in wonder than fright as the wooden pen came apart. "This is the first time I see San Francisco."

A well-born woman cursed her lily feet as she tried to flee the collapse of Chinatown.

A herd of buffalo breached the fences in Golden Gate Park, and thundered through Pacific Heights. Coming up against the bay, they turned south looking for a way home.

On Alcatraz, Pelican Island, men in ghost shirts for whom Wounded Knee was yesterday, ghost-danced out of cells and stole a boat to carry them away.

Then the fires began, and they were much worse than the shaking.

The business district was razed, every scrap of folding money, every stock certificate, or gold bond was incinerated.

Then, suddenly, the fires stopped.

At the doors of the Mission Dolores, some will tell you, Our Lady of Guadelupe, Madre de las Americas, says no more.

On the street where I once lived, I say.

Trying to Stay in Touch

February 11, 1898

Dear Mary Ellen,

You concern yourself too much about me. I thrive. Honest. Alone. And among my newfound friends.

My life is not as gloomy as it sounds. Nor as dead-ended. I came here—rather, I landed here out of the blue.

I do not want to inflate my experience like others I, and you, might name. I well know that I am not unique. No, I am unique, I remember my lessons. Rather, I am not extraordinary. I am a uniquely ordinary human being.

Why do I choose now to answer your letters? Well, I have tried before, and no doubt will later. Off and on I have written and the letters manage to get only as far as the layer of paper on which kindling rests. Whoosh! Gone.

I spent the years of the war on a Confederate chain gang. Is that revelation, explanation, enough?

Perhaps not.

I was chained, a man among men, until a guard spied a trickle of blood down my leg, and not from the chafing of the iron cuff.

You can imagine what happened next to me.

Maybe not.

Suffice to say, I was given my own chain, or should I say leash.

I was cuffed around the neck and led from man to man. They were not allowed to resist. We never made eye contact, not once.

We put on quite a show.

Chain against chain. Metal and flesh. The profoundly entertained keepers.

Memory.

There is a point of no return, I assure you.

I detached my nether parts from the rest of me. But I could not disown my mouth, the burning in my throat.

You can imagine.

We were set free when some Yankees came upon us, dispatched the keepers, and found a blacksmith, who with the proper blandishment dissolved another fellow's forgery.

I said nothing. I was stooped from the leash, and walked with my eyes drilling into the ground. I simply turned away from them, offered no thanks, and began to walk in the direction of my home. South.

And eventually I ended up here.

This is the point at which I usually twist the paper and lay it in the fireplace, even in the depths of the warm weather.

Like someone with an amputated limb, I can feel the cuff to this day. I respond to the tug of the chain.

There I was, my color long dissolved in springtime's torrents. There I was, a light-skinned woman on a leash. A thing of wonderment to some.

"She's no more a nigger than I am. What is she?" A woman friend of one of the keepers, come to enjoy the daily entertainment, asked.

Did she fear she might be next?

I don't think so.

I thought of Industry, the bit rusting in her mouth.

I thought of hurricane season, when the coconut palms bend and brush the ground. Industry standing beneath them. Industry walking into the sea, roiling in tempest. The waves smashing against the bit, but no power of nature equal to the task.

This is the story I do not tell.

Annie.

On a Sailboat off Cuttyhunk Island,
Sea Finally Calm

. . . remember me, . . . and if you remember not, O then I
will remind you of what you forget, how dear and beautiful
was the time we had together . . . no hill was there, nor holy
place, nor brook, whither we did not go.

"It does not do to mourn, Annie. Never," she said to
no one.

The lyric floated in her brain.

The ocean was impassive.

There were no ship tracks, no oceanic ruts where
they'd plowed, like the ruts across High Plains, High Desert, burned into the earth, rivulets of human passage, visible
from space.

And alongside the ruts, the odd grave. Of the woman
who was homesick and was taken suddenly, in her sleep; of

the child, dying because the milk cow grazed on Jamestown weed; of the man, by his own hand, suddenly frightened, and unwilling to threaten the enterprise. But these were few and far between, trace elements of the human greening the ground, a periwinkle blooming where nothing but Indian paintbrush was before.

O, Pioneers!

The ocean closed its books, darkness revealing nothing.

She'd met a man in a diving suit once, a daring fellow, ready to launch himself into San Francisco Bay. He told her the thing that impressed him was how quiet it was.

"Not a single sound."

Underneath, underneath right now the painting came to life. The stunning fish, the brown limbs, the chain.

In the darkness, in the silence at the bottom, bones comminuted into sand, midden becoming hourglass. Here and there a golden guinea shone, the coin minted fresh for the Trade, surface impressed by an African elephant. Bone into sand, into coral, alive, glancing against gold, growing into it, into the African elephant.

The sunlight on the surface of the water bathed her face.

She felt everyone behind her. In the here and now.

She'd returned to the Vineyard, to Cuttyhunk, where the Free African School had been, to walk through her childhood.

The school was decaying on a bluff above the ocean,

splinter by splinter falling into it. Not much left but a few beams, these a-tilt, with a residue of sea salt and evidence of shipworms.

The books were gone.

Miss Carey, the schoolmistress, had each of her students memorize, for recitation on command, a narrative in its entirety.

"Books are fragile things," she explained. "What they contain can easily be lost. We must become talking books; talk it on, like the Africans, children. Talk it on."

She was a strong-voiced woman. "Sarah?" She called out.

"Yes, Miss Carey."

"Please come forward to recite."

And Sarah began.

"I offer here neither the history of a saint, a hero, nor a tyrant. I believe there are few events in my life which have not happened to many, but when I compare my lot with that of many of my countrymen, I acknowledge the mercies of Providence in the occurrences that have taken place.

"I was kidnapped, I arrived at the seacoast, and I beheld that element, which before I had no idea of. The thing that met my sight was a slave ship, riding at anchor, waiting for her cargo. Her name was the *Good News.* I was taken on board . . ."

And Sarah continued, but Mary Ellen could no longer remember the rest of it.

Who had been hers?

"Mary Ellen?"

"Yes, ma'am."

"You may begin."

"In the year 1761, a little girl about seven or eight years old, I was stolen from my parents in Africa, and being put on board a ship, a passage I can barely remember, was brought to Boston, where I was sold for a slave. I soon learned the English language and in about a year I could read it perfectly. I taught myself to write.

"A small volume of my verse was published, in which the following advertisement appears. 'We, whose names are underwritten, do assure the world that the Poems specified in the following pages were, as we verily believe, written by Phillis, a young Negro girl who but a few years ago was brought here, an uncultivated barbarian, and has ever since been, and now is, under the disadvantage of serving as a slave in a family in this town. She has been examined by some of the best judges, and is thought qualified to write them . . .'"

It was in the schoolhouse that she heard of Quasheba's death, there that the ceremony was held. She felt someone placing the gun in her hands.

"Are you ready?" he asked her.

"I am ready," she responded.

"Prepare to accept your mother's arms."

"I am prepared."

She felt everyone behind her.

They should all be resting together.

But only Quasheba's grave was known to her. In the sandy ground, rescued from the Maroon encampment in the Great Dismal Swamp, brought here in a burlap sack, buried deep beneath a sand dune.

Captain Parsons dreamed somewhere in darkest Africa, his bones dusting trails blazed and gazetted by the likes of Livingstone, Stanley.

And she, their belovéd daughter, would one day abide in Napa, overwhelmed by a white oleander, arched by the thorns and fruit of a wild blackberry bush, each growing from her. The berries in season staining the white marble of her gravestone, the black juice running into the letters she chose,

SHE WAS A FRIEND OF JOHN BROWN

She is at the tiller of a rented boat. Gulls follow in her wake, close enough she can make out the red spot on the yellow beak. Target for the chicks. She scattered some bread in the wake to encourage them.

They accept her offerings, stay with her, then, with a squawk and a clatter of wings, dive into the water and emerge with huge, blue-tinted clams, which they drop onto the rocks at the island's edge, diving this time for the sweet and wet and salty being separated from its shell.

A midden grew as monument to their ingenuity.